ROMAN HISTORY AND COINAGE 44 BC–AD 69

Fifty Points of Relation from Julius Caesar to Vespasian

C. H. V. SUTHERLAND

D1091943

CLARENDON PRESS · OXFORD

1987

Oxford University Press, Walton Street, Oxford OX2 6DP
Oxford New York Toronto
Delhi Bombay Calcutta Madras Karachi
Petaling Jaya Singapore Hong Kong Tokyo
Nairobi Dar es Salaam Cape Town
Melbourne Auckland
and associated companies in
Beirut Berlin Ibadan Nicosia

Oxford is a trade mark of Oxford University Press

Published in the United States
by Oxford University Press, New York

© C. H. V. Sutherland 1987

All rights reserved. No part of this publication may be reproduced,
stored in a retrieval system, or transmitted, in any form or by any means,
electronic, mechanical, photocopying, recording, or otherwise, without
the prior permission of Oxford University Press

This book is sold subject to the condition that it shall not, by way
of trade or otherwise, be lent, re-sold, hired out or otherwise circulated
without the publisher's prior consent in any form of binding or cover
other than that in which it is published and without a similar condition
including this condition being imposed on the subsequent purchaser

British Library Cataloguing in Publication Data
Sutherland, C. H. V.
Roman history and coinage, 44 BC–AD 69:
fifty points of relation from Julius Caesar to Vespasian.
1. Coins, Roman
I. Title
737.4937'09'014   CJ833
ISBN–19–872124–2
ISBN 0–19–872123–4 Pbk

Library of Congress Cataloging in Publication Data
Sutherland, C. H. V. (Carol Humphrey Vivian), 1908–
Roman history and coinage, 44 BC–AD 69.
Bibliography: p.
Includes index.
1. Coins, Roman.   2. Rome—History—Civil War,
43–31 B.C.   3. Rome—History—The five Julii, 30 B.C.—
68 A.D.   I. Title.
CJ1001.S76 1986   737. 4937   86–18165
ISBN 0–19–872124–2
ISBN 0–19–872123–4 (pbk.)

Set by Joshua Associates Ltd., Oxford
Printed in Great Britain
at the University Printing House, Oxford
by David Stanford
Printer to the University

PREFACE

MOST modern histories of the early Roman empire, and most of the commentaries on the relevant ancient texts, refer only summarily and uncritically to the evidence, complementary or supplementary, furnished by the imperial coinage (though Dr Griffin's *Nero* is a notable exception). Similarly, books on the early imperial coinage seldom cite the relevant passages of the ancient historians in any critically revealing way. As a result, students of the earlier empire—that period covered primarily by Augustus' *Res Gestae*, Velleius Paterculus, Tacitus, Suetonius, Plutarch, and Dio Cassius—have tended to approach the evidence of the coinage warily. They find in the major coin-catalogues an immense variety of coins in a rigorously structured arrangement, a form which historians have indeed often required of them. And they are aware of some failure in the matching or comparing or opposing of literary evidence (the work of private individuals) with numismatic evidence (the result of government agency).

It therefore seems worth while, by way of a new approach, to select from this richly documented period a series of historical passages with which the evidence of coins is necessarily involved. Primary attention is given to the historians: only then is the associated numismatic evidence examined. This book is not 'Numismatic documents of the early empire'. It seeks, quite simply, to illustrate a close if intermittent parallelism. I was encouraged to persevere in this comparative experiment by Dr Barbara Levick, Fellow of St Hilda's College, Oxford. With great kindness and a very keen eye she read the preliminary draft, and she has helped me to reduce the number of residual errors which must be laid to my account. At a later stage, moreover, and with equal generosity, she strengthened many passages of discussion by appropriate reference to the recent and most important critical work of modern historians of the Roman empire. I here express to her my warmest thanks for her invaluable help.

This book does not attempt to tread on the controversial

ground of the purpose of imperial coin-types. My views on this question have already been expressed, with some development of emphasis, in *JRS* 1959, pp. 46ff., and *Rev. Num.* 1983, pp. 73ff. The imperial coinage was, fundamentally, a government-controlled economic instrument which also said things, and usually illustrated them. This much is beyond question or denial.

The coins cited in the following pages are in nearly all cases referenced according to *Roman Imperial Coinage*, vol. I, revised edition, 1984 (cited as *RIC* I²). This includes illustrations of many of the coins in question, and also gives references to the British Museum and other catalogues where many more are illustrated.

Because a knowledge of Greek, and even of Latin, is now less common than it used to be, translations are provided of the historical passages quoted from the ancient authors. And I have, throughout, amplified the coin-legends, in many of which severe abbreviation was normal as a means of saving space in the very small area available.

Finally, I have to express my warm gratitude to those museums which have so kindly provided me with plaster casts of the coins to be illustrated. Most are derived from the British Museum, with additions from Berlin, Vienna, and the Ashmolean at Oxford.

C.H.V.S.

Cumnor, Oxford,
September 1985

CJ
1001
.597
1987

CONTENTS

SELECT BIBLIOGRAPHY

Short titles appear in bold print following entries.

Balsdon, J. P. V. D., *The Emperor Gaius* (Oxford, 1934) (**Gaius**)

Brunt, P. A., and Moore, J. M., *Res Gestae divi Augusti: The Achievements of the Divine Augustus* (Oxford, 1967)

Campbell, J. B., *The emperor and the Roman Army, 31 BC–AD 235* (Oxford, 1984) (**ERA**)

Crawford, M. H., *Roman Republican Coinage* (Cambridge, 1974) (**RRC**)

—— *Roman Republican Coin Hoards* (London, 1969) (**RRCH**)

Dreis, H., *Die Cohortes Urbanae* (Cologne and Graz, 1967) (**CU**)

Gagé, J., *Res Gestae Divi Augusti* (Paris, 1935) (**RGDA**)

Grant, M., *From Imperium to Auctoritas* (Cambridge, 1946) (**FITA**)

—— *Roman Anniversary Issues* (Cambridge, 1950) (**RAI**)

—— *The Six Main Aes Coinages of Augustus* (Edinburgh, 1953) (**SMACA**)

Grenade, P., *Essai sur les origines du principat* (Paris, 1961) (**EOP**)

Griffin, M. T., *Nero, the End of a Dynasty* (London, 1984) (**Nero**)

—— *Seneca, a Philosopher in Politics* (Oxford, 1976) (**Seneca**)

Hennig, D., *L. Aelius Seianus* (Munich, 1975) (**Seianus**)

Jullian, C., *Histoire de la Gaule* IV (Paris, 1913) (**HG**)

Levick, B., *Tiberius the Politician* (London, 1976) (**TP**)

—— (ed.), *The Ancient Historian and his Materials* (Farnborough, 1976) (**AHM**)

Liebeschuetz, J. H. W. G., *Continuity and Change in Roman Religion* (Oxford, 1979) (**CCRR**)

Magdelain, A., *Auctoritas Principis* (Paris, 1945) (**AP**)

Magie, D., *Roman Rule in Asia Minor* (Princeton, 1950) (**RRAM**)

Meiggs, R., *Roman Ostia* (ed. 2, Oxford, 1973) (**Ostia**)

Millar, F., *The Emperor in the Roman World* (London, 1977) (**ERW**)

Pauly–Wissowa, *Real-Encyclopädie der classischen Altertumswissenschaft* (**RE**)

Princeton Encyclopedia of Ancient Sites (Princeton, 1978)

Reinhold, M., *Marcus Agrippa* (New York, 1933; repr. Rome, 1965) (**Agrippa**)

Rickman, G., *The Corn Supply of Ancient Rome* (Oxford, 1980) (**CSAR**)

Rodewald, C., *Money in the Age of Tiberius* (Manchester, 1976) (**MAT**)

Rogers, R. S., *Studies in the Reign of Tiberius* (Baltimore, 1943) (**SRT**)

Seager, R., *Tiberius* (London, 1972) (**Tiberius**)

Sherwin-White, A. N., *Roman Foreign Policy in the East, 168 BC–AD 1* (London, 1984) (**RFPE**)

Smallwood, E. M., *Documents illustrating the Principates of Gaius, Claudius and Nero* (Cambridge, 1967)

Sutherland, C. H. V., *Coinage and Currency in Roman Britain* (London, 1937) (**CCRB**)

—— *The Romans in Spain* (London, 1939) (**RS**)

—— *Gold* (London, 1959) (**Gold**)

—— *Coinage in Roman Imperial Policy* (London, 1951; repr. London and New York, 1971) (**CRIP**)

—— *The Cistophori of Augustus* (London, 1970) (**CA**)

—— *The Emperor and the Coinage: Julio-Claudian Studies* (London, 1976) (**EC**)

Syme, R., *The Roman Revolution* (Oxford, 1939) (**RR**)

Van Berchem, D., *Les Distributions de blé et de l'argent à la plèbe romaine dans l'empire* (Geneva, 1939; repr. Rome, 1979) (**DBA**)

Weinstock, S., *Divus Iulius* (Oxford, 1971) (**DI**)

Woodman, A. J., *Velleius Paterculus: the Tiberian Narrative* (Cambridge, 1977)

Ziegler, K.-H., *Die Beziehungen zwischen Rom and der Partherreich* (Wiesbaden, 1964) (**BRP**)

ABBREVIATIONS

AJPhil	*American Journal of Philology*
Antiqu. Journ.	*Antiquaries Journal*
BAR	*British Archaeological Reports*
BMC	British Museum *Catalogue of Greek Coins*
BMCRE I	*British Museum Catalogue of Coins of the Roman Empire* I (London, 1923)
CAH	*Cambridge Ancient History*
CIL	*Corpus Inscriptionum Latinarum* (Berlin, 1863–)
CQ	*Classical Quarterly*
Class. Rev.	*Classical Review*
Dio Cass.	Dio Cassius
E. and J.[2]	Ehrenberg, V., and Jones, A. H. M., *Documents Illustrating the Reigns of Augustus and Tiberius* (ed. 2, Oxford, 1955)
Essays . . . Mattingly	*Essays in Roman Coinage Presented to Harold Mattingly*, ed. Carson, R. A. G., and Sutherland, C. H. V. (Oxford, 1956)
Fast. Amit.	See Gagé, J., *Res Gestae Divi Augusti* (Paris, 1935), pp. 160 ff.
— *Ant.*	
— *Barb.*	
— *Cum.*	
— *Maff.*	
— *Praen.*	
— *Vat.*	
Fragm. Hist. Graec.	*Fragmenta Historicorum Graecorum*, ed. Müller (Paris, 1841–72)
Hist.	*Historia*
ILS	Dessau, H., *Inscriptiones Latinae Selectae* (Berlin, 1892–1916)
Jahrb. für Num. und Geldgesch.	*Jahrbuch für Numismatik und Geldgeschichte*
JRS	*Journal of Roman Studies*
Mem. Amer. Acad. Rome	*Memoirs of the American Academy in Rome*
NACQT	*Numismatica e Antichità Classiche, Quaderni Ticinesi*
Num. Chron.	*Numismatic Chronicle*

Num. Zeitschr.	*Numismatische Zeitschrift*
PBSR	*Papers of the British School at Rome*
PIR	*Prosopographia Imperii Romani* (Berlin, 1897–8 and 1933–)
Plin. *Epist.*	Pliny the younger, *Epistles*
Plin. *NH*	Pliny the elder, *Natural History*
Plut.	Plutarch
Rev. Belge	*Revue belge de numismatique*
Rev. Num.	*Revue numismatique*
RG	*Res Gestae Divi Augusti*
RIC I²	*Roman Imperial Coinage* I (ed. 2, London, 1984)
Scripta . . . Sutherland	*Scripta Nummaria Romana: Essays presented to Humphrey Sutherland*, ed. Carson, R. A. G., and Kraay, C. M. (London, 1978)
Suet.	Suetonius
Tac. *Ann.*, *Hist.*	Tacitus, *Annals* and *Histories*
Vell. Pat.	Velleius Paterculus

THE IMPERIAL MONETARY SYSTEM ESTABLISHED FROM AUGUSTUS ONWARDS

1 gold aureus	=	25 silver denarii
1 silver denarius	=	16 copper asses
1 brass sestertius	=	4 copper asses
1 brass dupondius	=	2 copper asses
1 copper as	=	2 copper semisses (or 4 copper quadrantes)

See in general *RIC* I², pp. 3 and 23. Note that the use of the term *aes* in the following pages covers, loosely but conventionally, coinage of brass as well as of copper.

1. Julius Caesar's control of the *aerarium* and the mint of Rome

1. Suet. *Div. Iul.* 76. 2 f. Tertium et quartum consulatum titulo tenus gessit contentus dictaturae potestate decretae cum consulatibus simul atque utroque anno binos consules substituit sibi in ternos novissimos menses ... Pridie autem Kalendas Ianuarias repentina consulis morte cessantem honorem in paucas horas petenti dedit. Eadem licentia spreto patrio more magistratus in pluris annos ordinavit ... Praeterea monetae publicisque vectigalibus peculiares servos praeposuit.

Suet. *Div. Iul.* 76. 2 f. Caesar held his third and fourth consulships in name only, being content with the power of the dictatorship voted to him with the consulships, and in each of those two consular years he appointed two consuls as substitutes for himself for the last three months ... When a consul died suddenly on the day before 1 January he bestowed the office, vacant for the few remaining hours, on a man who sought it. He spurned tradition with the same abandon by appointing magistrates for several years in advance ... Moreover he placed his household slaves in charge of the mint and the public taxes.

1b　　　*1c*

a Crawford, *RRC*, p. 478, no. 466. 1. Aureus of Rome, 46 BC. *Obv.* C
   CAESAR COS (*consul*) TER(*tium*), Head of Pietas. *Rev.* A HIR-
   TIVS PR(*aetor?*), Lituus, jug, and axe.

b Crawford, *RRC*, p. 485, no. 475. 1a. Aureus of Rome, 45 BC. *Obv.*
   C CAESAR DIC(*tator*) TER(*tium*), Bust of Victory. *Rev.* L
   PLANC(*us*) PRAEF(*ectus*) VRB(*is*), Jug.

c Crawford, *RRC*, p. 488, no. 480. 2a. Denarius of Rome, *c.* January
   44 BC. *Obv.* CAESAR DICT(*ator*) QVART(*um*), Caesar's head,
   laureate. *Rev.* M METTIVS, Juno in biga.

d Crawford, *RRC*, p. 489, no. 480. 7b. Denarius of Rome, *c.* Febru-
   ary 44 BC. *Obv.* CAESAR DICT(*ator*) PERPETVO, Caesar's head,
   laureate. *Rev.* L BVCA, Venus seated holding Victory and sceptre.

Until the time of Julius Caesar the *aerarium Saturni*, the public
treasury of the Roman state, had been controlled by the
quaestors on behalf of the senate, and the technical day-to-day
operation of the mint of Rome, established in the temple of
Juno Moneta (from which the derivation of 'money'), had been
the responsibility of the *tresviri aere argento auro flando feriundo*, a
section of what was then the body of the annual vigintisexvir-
ate, young aspirants to the senate. The tresviri *a. a. a. f. f.*
formed an annual *collegium* which supervised the production of
coinage, in the quantity and the metal(s) required by the
aerarium, for the discharge of its obligations. Suetonius (*Div.
Iul.* 76. 1) recorded the steady growth of Caesar's powers after
his Gallic campaign, culminating in the *dictatura perpetua*, the
praefectura morum, the *praenomen imperatoris*, and the cognomen
pater patriae, and went on to say that Caesar took control of the
mint and of the public taxes (i.e. the *aerarium*) by the simple
expedient of placing them in the hands of his personal servants.
With his control of coinage-metals thus assured he could coin
according to his own wishes. In 46 and 45 BC his orders to the
mint were transmitted directly through A. Hirtius and L. Plancus, respectively *praetor*(?) and *praefectus urbis*, for the coinage of
large quantities of gold, presumably to repay his debts and to
defray the costs of his recent triumph. The coinages of the most
prominent of the native communities in Gaul had included
many issues of gold (cf. D. Nash in *Scripta . . . Sutherland*,
pp. 12 f.), and in conformity with common ancient practice
Caesar would have turned this into current Roman coin: the

quantity of the newly acquired gold, moreover, would have prompted him to lower the weight of the aureus from the nearly 11 g of Sulla and the *c*.9 g of Pompey to just over 8 g. In 44 BC he appointed *quattuorviri* instead of *tresviri* to run the mint: their names—M. Mettius, L. Aemilius Buca, P. Sepullius Macer, and C. Cossutius Maridianus—are to be seen on the common denarii of that year, the later of which (cf. C. M. Kraay in *Num. Chron.* 1954, pp. 19 ff.) were struck after Caesar's death, showing a veiled portrait. All the coin-portraits of 44 BC show Caesar wearing the laurel-wreath with which (Suet. *Div. Iul.* 45. 2) he was said to have gladly concealed his receding hair-line.

There is no reason to suppose that the control of the mint of Rome, once it had been assumed by Caesar (for whom it was aptly underlined by the Juno reverse of M. Mettius), ever returned effectively into senatorial hands, save perhaps briefly during Nero's first decade as *princeps* (see no. **36**). Moreover, Caesar's control of the *aerarium* from *c*.46 BC resulted in a subsequent ambiguity about its position *vis-à-vis* the state which Augustus was at no pains to clarify (see nos. **11** and **14**): although he did not put his slaves and freedmen in charge of the *aerarium*, he did use them in keeping abreast of its accounts (Suet. *Div. Aug.* 101). His control of imperial finances was by means of gifts (*RG* 17. 1; Brunt and Moore ad loc.). Later emperors were content to translate this ambiguity into increasing imperial control.

2. Octavian, *ultor* and *vindex libertatis*

1. *RG* 1. 1. Anno undeviginti natus exercitum privato consilio et privata impensa comparavi per quem rem publicam a dominatione factionis oppressam in libertatem vindicavi.

2. *RG* 2. Qui parentem meum trucidaverunt, eos in exilium expuli iudiciis legitimis ultus eorum facinus et postea bellum inferentis rei publicae vici bis acie.

RG 1. 1. At the age of nineteen I took the personal decision to raise an army from my private funds. With it I freed the state from the tyranny of faction.

RG 2. Those who had butchered my father I drove into exile, and justly avenged their crime, and later I twice defeated in battle those who were making war on the state.

2a   **2b**

a *RIC I²*, p. 79, no. 476. Cistophoric tetradrachm of Ephesus, 28 BC. *Obv.* IMP(*erator*) CAESAR DIVI F(*ilius*) COS VI LIBERTATIS P(*opuli*) R(*omani*) VINDEX, Head of Octavian, laureate. *Rev.* PAX, Pax standing with caduceus; beside her, snake emerging from *cista mystica*; all in laurel-wreath.

b *RIC* I², p. 43, no. 28. Aureus of 'uncertain Spanish mint', *c.*19–18 BC. *Obv.* AVGVSTVS, Head of Augustus, bare. *Rev.* MARTIS VLTORIS, Round temple with four columns containing figure of Mars standing holding aquila and standard.

Vengeance upon Caesar's murderers was swiftly sought by Octavian, and was achieved on 23 October 42 BC (*Fast. Praen.*) after the double victory (Suet. *Div. Aug.* 13. 1) at Philippi over Cassius and Brutus, later to be frankly argued (Tac. *Ann.* 1. 9) as a lawful act of retribution. *Ultio* having been achieved by war, the cult of Mars Ultor, the Avenger (for which see Weinstock, *DI*, pp. 128–32, there connected with Parthian expeditions), was instituted at Philippi in 42 BC with the vowing of a temple to him at Rome. This, with its accompanying *forum*

Augusti (for which see P. Zanker, *Forum Augustum: das Bild-programm*, Tübingen, n.d. [1969]), was not inaugurated until 1 August 2 BC (*RG* 21. 1; Dio Cass. 60. 5. 3; Vell. Pat. 2. 100). But much earlier coin types of a small, circular temple of Mars Ultor were frequent at the two unidentified mints hitherto attri-buted with some reason to Spain (*RIC* I², pp. 25 ff., 43 ff.), though these types were not employed at Rome or Lugdunum. As these coin types show, it was in this small temple that the standards restored by Parthia in 20 BC (*RG* 29. 2; cf. no. 6) were first ceremonially laid up, until their transference to the new and larger temple in 2 BC.

The concept of Octavian as *vindex*—the champion of the liberty of others (cf. no. 43)—is seen on the silver tetradrachms (= 3 denarii) most probably struck at Ephesus in the province of Asia (Sutherland, *The Cistophori of Augustus*, pp. 12 ff., 85 ff.) in 28 BC (COS VI). These, styling him *libertatis p. R. vindex*, allude specifically to the liberation of Asia from the domination of Antony, and more generally to the parallel liberation of the whole *res publica* through the victory at Actium. *Asia Recepta* appeared as the reverse legend, accompanied by a Victory type, on a very large issue of silver quinarii (= half-denarii) struck between 29 and 26 BC (IMP VIII) most probably at an Italian mint that preceded the reopening of the mint of Rome (*RIC* I², pp. 31, 61). The essence of the victory in Asia lay in the act of recovery.

3. Octavian, Egypt, and the East

1. *RG* 27. 1 f. Aegyptum imperio populi Romani adieci. Armeniam maiorem interfecto rege eius Artaxe cum possem facere provinciam malui maiorum nostrorum exemplo regnum id Tigrani . . . tradere.

RG 27. 1 f. I added Egypt to the empire of the Roman people. When Artaxes, king of greater Armenia, had been killed, I could have formed a province, but I preferred to follow tradition and hand over the territory as a kingdom to Tigranes.

3b   *3c*

a *RIC* I², p. 61, no. 275. Denarius of Italy(?). *Obv.* CAESAR COS VI
   (= 28 BC), Octavian's head, bare; lituus behind. *Rev.* AEGVPTO
   CAPTA, Crocodile.

b *RIC* I², p. 86, nos. 544f. Aureus and denarius, uncertain mint.
   Obv. CAESAR DIVI F(*ilius*) COS VI or VII (28, 27 BC), Augustus'
   head, bare; small capricorn below. *Rev.* AEGVPT(O) CAPTA,
   Crocodile.

c *RIC* I², p. 83, no. 514. Aureus of Pergamum, *c*.19–18 BC. *Obv.*
   AVGVSTVS, Augustus' head, bare. *Rev.* ARMENIA CAPTA,
   Victory cutting bull's throat.

d *RIC* I², p. 83, no. 518. Denarius of Pergamum. *Obv.* Augustus'
   head, bare. *Rev.* CAESAR DIVI F(*ilius*) ARMEN(*ia*) RECE(*pta*)
   IMP VIIII (= 20 BC), Armenian standing with spear and bow.

On 1 August 30 BC (*Fast. Praen.*) Octavian added Egypt to the
dominions of Rome by the capture of Alexandria. Egypt was
not, however, to be a normal province, for it was governed
henceforth by a series of imperially appointed *praefecti* capable
of safeguarding the rich treasure of its annual grain-harvest (see
P. A. Brunt in *JRS* 1975, pp. 124–47). *Aegypto Capta* appeared
as a coin-type in the early twenties BC, at unidentified mints. It
was never employed at the major western mints of Augustus in
Spain or Gaul, or at Rome itself. The anomalous status, or
perhaps more specifically the anomalous government, of the
newly captured territory may have caused this apparently
deliberate omission: the taking of Alexandria had, after all,
provided one day of the three-day triumph of 29 BC (Suet. *Div.*

Aug. 22; Dio Cass. 51. 21; *Fast. Barb.* under 13–15 August). Perhaps, too, there was something less than fully glorious in the capture of territory bequeathed fifty years earlier and now put out of bounds to senators and *equites* without special permission: reasons for the special treatment of Egypt are discussed by Brunt and Moore on *RG* 27.1 f. The same note of reserve may possibly be felt in Augustus' reference to Armenia (for which see Brunt and Moore on *RG* 27. 2; J. G. C. Anderson, *CAH* x, ch. 9; and Magie, *RRAM*, p. 476). The conversion of this area into a client kingdom under Tigranes received only passing numismatic record. Pergamum alone referred to it, on the Roman-weight coinage of gold and silver issued there *c.* 19–18 BC, presumably for the pay of the Roman forces which had produced the Parthian concessions of 20 BC (*Rev. Num.* 1973, pp. 129 ff.).

4. The title *Augustus*, and *auctoritas*

1. *RG* 34. In consulatu sexto et septimo, postquam bella civilia extinxeram, per consensum universorum potitus rerum omnium, rem publicam ex mea potestate in senatus populique Romani arbitrium transtuli. Quo pro merito meo senatus consulto Augustus appellatus sum, et laureis postes aedium mearum vestiti publice, coronaque civica super ianuam meam fixa est et clupeus aureus in curia Iulia positus quem mihi senatum populumque Romanum dare virtutis clementiaeque iustitiae et pietatis caussa testatum est per eius clupei inscriptionem. Post id tempus auctoritate omnibus praestiti, potestatis autem nihilo amplius habui quam ceteri qui mihi quoque in magistratu conlegae fuerunt.

RG 34. In my sixth and seventh consulships, when I had stamped out all civil warfare and was by universal consent master of all, I transferred the state from my absolute power to the free authority of the senate and people of Rome. In deserving recognition of this I was named Augustus by decree of the senate, my door-posts were publicly hung with laurels, a civic crown was fixed above the door, and a golden shield was placed in the Curia Julia, the inscription on which testified that it was a gift from the senate and people of Rome on account of my valour, clemency, justice, and sense of duty. After that I possessed authority greater than that of all others, but power greater than none of those who were colleagues with me in any magistracy.

4b   4c

a *RIC* I², p. 73, no. 413. Aureus of Rome, 12 BC. *Obv.* AVGVSTVS DIVI F(*ilius*), Augustus' head, bare. *Rev.* (?) COSSVS LENTVLVS RES PVB(*lica*) AVGVST(*us*), Augustus, in toga, extending hand to kneeling Respublica.

b *RIC* I², p. 74, no. 419. Aureus of Rome, 12 BC. *Obv.* AVGVSTVS DIVI F, Augustus' head, bare. *Rev.* L CANINIVS GALLVS OB C(*ives*) S(*ervatos*), Oak-wreath above closed double door flanked by laurel-branches.

c *RIC* I², p. 44, no. 42b. Denarius of 'uncertain Spanish mint 1', *c.*19–18 BC. *Obv.* CAESAR AVGVSTVS, Augustus' head, bare. *Rev.* S P Q R / CL V in two lines on shield.

d *RIC* I², p. 73, no. 406. Denarius of Rome, 13 BC. *Obv.* CAESAR AVGVSTVS, Augustus' head, bare. *Rev.* C SVLPIC(*ius*) PLAT-ORIN(*us*), Augustus and Agrippa, each wearing toga, seated on rostral platform; upright spear beside them.

Augustus' formal renunciation of *potestas*, power without constitutional limits, and his declared return to republican constitutionalism, took place in 28–27 BC (for the events of these years see Grenade, *EOP* pp. 144–81). In 28 the illegalities of the late triumvirate were annulled (cf. Dio Cass. 53. 2. 5), and on 13 January 27 (*Fast. Praen.*; cf. Ovid, *Fasti* 1. 589) the provinces were restored to the administration of the senate and people, who in turn handed some back to Augustus. On the same day the senate decreed that the *corona civica*, the oak-wreath awarded *ob cives servatos*, should be fixed above the door of his house, where triumphal laurels (mentioned by *RG*, and shown on coins, but not specified in the *Fasti*) were also displayed. Three days later, on 16 January 27 (*Fast. Cum.* and *Praen.*; cf. Ovid *Fasti* 1. 589, by error under 13 January), he accepted the half-name, half-title *Augustus* (Suet. *Div. Aug.* 7; Vell. Pat. 2. 91), with its augural overtone: this style was henceforth to be dominant on his coinage throughout the Roman world. At a date not recorded, the senate and people caused a golden shield to be erected in the Curia Julia (the senate-house), near to the statue and altar of Victory dedicated there on 28 August 29 BC (*Fast. Maff.* and *Vat.*; cf. Dio Cass. 51. 22. 1), as a result of which coins often show the shield and the figure of Victory in very close association (*RIC* I², p. 47, no. 90; p. 48, no. 93; p. 64, no. 321). The shield was public testimony to Augustus' four primary qualities as *princeps*—*virtus*, *clementia*, *iustitia*, and *pietas*; and the ceremonies of January 27 BC, taken as a whole, were intended as a public acknowledgement of the 'restoration' of the Republic (cf. Livy, *Per.* 134; Vell. Pat. 2. 89. For changing views on Augustus' constitutional position see G. E. F. Chilver in *Historia* 1950, pp. 408–35: the concept of a restored Republic has been critically assessed more recently by E. A. Judge in *Polis and Imperium*, ed. J. A. S. Evans (Toronto, 1972), pp. 279–311, and F. Millar in *JRS* 1973, pp. 50–67. For the ceremonies of 27 BC see W. K. Lacey in *JRS* 1974, pp. 176–84). From 27 until 23 Augustus still retained supreme military *imperium*, which he chose to regard, questionably, as a consequence of his continuing series of consulships (VII–XI) in those years; from 23, abandoning the consulship, he enjoyed *imperium maius*. Neither was mentioned in *RG*. Nevertheless it was true that he had restored collegiate magistracy—he is shown on coinage (*d*) as a colleague with Agrippa in *tribunicia potestas*—and he had acquired supreme *auctoritas* (see Magdelain, *AP*): Dio Cassius (53. 18) contrasts the new ἀξίωμα (the term used in the Monumentum Ancyranum) with the former δύναμις. Because *auctoritas* was not a formal power, but connoted simply unrivalled influence, it received no epigraphic or numismatic reflection: the interpretation of C A on eastern bronze coinage as *Caesaris auctoritate*

(Grant, *FITA*, p. 108) has not received general support, for *Commune Asiae* is so much more probable. Regarded as a whole, however, Augustus' coinage does clearly reflect his immensely powerful personal position at the centre of government. The now very rare aureus of 12 BC (*a*) showing him in the act of raising a kneeling Respublica neatly encapsulates his achievement; and denarii of 16 BC (*RIC* I², p. 68, no. 358) show a remarkably expressive obverse legend reading I(*ovi*) O(*ptimo*) M(*aximo*) S P Q R PR(*o*) S(*alute*) IMP(*eratoris*) CAE(*saris*) QVOD PER EV(*m*) R(*es*) P(*ublica*) IN AMP(*liore*) AT Q(*ue*) TRA*(quilliore*) S(*tatu*) E(*st*). The ceremonies of January 27 BC were commemorated by Vespasian exactly one hundred years later (Grant, *RAI*, pp. 88 ff.).

5. Augustus and the silver statuary

1. *RG* 24. 2. Statuae meae pedestres et equestres et in quadrigeis argenteae steterunt in urbe XXC circiter, quas ipse sustuli exque ea pecunia dona aurea in aede Apollinis meo nomine et illorum qui mihi statuarum honorem habuerunt posui.

2. Suet. *Div. Aug.* 52. Templa, quamvis sciret etiam proconsulibus decerni solere, in nulla tamen provincia nisi communi suo Romaeque nomine recepit. Nam in urbe quidem pertinacissime abstinuit hoc honore; atque etiam argenteas statuas olim sibi positas conflavit omnis exque iis aureas cortinas Apollini Palatio dedicavit.

3. Dio Cass. 53. 22. ὁ Αὔγουστος καὶ ἀνδριάντας τινὰς ἑαυτοῦ ἀργυροῦς ... ἐς νόμισμα κατέκοψε. (Of 27 BC.)

RG 24. 2: There were in Rome about 80 silver statues of me, either standing or mounted on horseback or in four-horse chariots. These I removed, and from the money they provided I placed gifts of gold in the temple of Apollo, in my name and in the name of those who had set up the statues in my honour.

Suet. *Div. Aug.* 52. Augustus knew that it was customary for temples to be decreed even to proconsuls, but he accepted no such honour for himself unless it was jointly in his name and that of Rome. In Rome itself he set his face against any such honour, and even melted down all the silver statues of himself set up there, dedicating from the proceeds golden tripods to the Palatine Apollo.

Dio Cass. 53. 22. Augustus also struck coinage from various silver statues of himself.

5a   5b

a *RIC* I², p. 61, no. 275. Denarius of Italy or Rome. *Obv.* CAESAR COS VI (28 BC), Octavian's head, bare; lituus behind. *Rev.* AEGVPTO CAPTA, Crocodile.

b *RIC* I², p. 61, no. 276. Quinarius (= half-denarius) of Italy or Rome. *Obv.* CAESAR IMP(*erator*) VII (29–26 BC), Octavian's head, bare. *Rev.* ASIA RECEPTA, Victory on *cista mystica* between two snakes.

Three sources, one of them Augustus himself, and one dated to 27 BC, record that Augustus melted down a number of silver statues of himself in Rome, 'about 80' of them, as he said. Whether these were of solid silver, or silver-plated, is nowhere specified. Nor is his reason for the action given. Suetonius, after stating that in the provinces Augustus permitted temples to himself only in the joint names of *Roma et Augustus* (cf. *RIC* I², p. 82, nos. 505f., mint of Pergamum), added after an ambiguous *nam* that he abstained as a matter of set habit from the principle of allowing honorific statues of himself in Rome. Dio Cassius says that he struck coinage (i.e. of silver) from the statues which were melted down, a statement rejected by Millar (*ERW*, p. 146) as a 'misunderstanding'. Augustus noted that from the money (*pecunia*) thus obtained he dedicated golden gifts (tripod-lebetes, according to Suetonius) in the temple of the Palatine Apollo (for Augustus and Apollo see now Liebeschuetz, *CCRR*, pp. 82–7). It is possible that Augustus, as a result of his capture of the royal treasure of Egypt (a land well known for its relative abundance of natural gold and its scarcity of natural silver; cf. Sutherland, *Gold*, pp. 26 ff.), found himself the possessor of a disproportionately large amount of gold: this may be reflected, for instance, in the 16,000 pounds weight of gold which he gave to the temple of the Capitoline Jupiter (Suet. *Div. Aug.* 30. 2; no date specified), a weight equivalent in coinage to some 640,000 aurei (for Carter on Suet. *Div. Aug.* ad loc. the Suetonian figures are 'exaggerated'). From an economic point of view, therefore, his action in regard to the silver statues may have been intended to lessen the disproportion, enabling him to coin more silver denarii (at 25 to the aureus; Dio Cass. 55. 12) than would otherwise have been possible. There is, however, one difficulty in this view. If Dio Cassius' date of 27 BC for the transformation of silver statues into silver coinage is correct, this would indeed enable us to suppose that with this silver coinage Augustus could have bought gold for the temple of the Capitoline Jupiter—a means of immobilizing some of the excess stock of gold and increasing the currency-stock of silver. Nevertheless, no substantial coinage of denarii can be assigned to Rome (or to any other western mint) *c.*27–26 BC. Relatively scarce denarii with a suitable *Aegypto Capta* reverse were struck in Italy or Rome in 28 BC, and large numbers of silver quinarii (half-denarii) with *Asia Recepta*—a less appropriate legend—between 29 and 26 BC. According to current theory, no extensive coinage of denarii was issued at Rome until *c.*19 BC, when the *tresviri monetales* P. Petronius Turpilianus, L. Aquillius Florus, and M. Durmius, assisted by Q. Rustius, struck a very large series, not individually abundant, but very abundant in the aggregate (*RIC* I², pp. 61 ff.). It is, of course, open to us to suppose that Augustus simply stock-piled a large quantity of the newly acquired Egyptian gold as a convenient reserve, or, however doubtfully, that the melting down of some 80 silver statues, of varying degrees of fineness, called for a process of assaying and refining which lasted for some years before the mint of Rome was ready for reopening and full production. This does not seem likely; and it must be concluded that the still abundant stocks of republican silver coinage, together with the copious denarii struck for Octavian in Italy down to 27 BC (cf. Crawford, *RRCH* pp. 117 ff.; *RIC* I², pp. 59 ff.), would have been quite enough for the normal needs of the Roman economy, and even perhaps for abnormal purchases of gold.

6. Augustus, Parthia, and the return of the standards

1. *RG* 29. 2. Parthos trium exercitum Romanorum spolia et signa reddere mihi supplicesque amicitiam populi Romani petere coegi.

2. Suet. *Div. Aug.* 21. 3. Parthi quoque et Armeniam vindicanti facile cesserunt et signa militaria, quae M. Crasso et M. Antonio ademerant, reposcenti reddiderunt obsidesque insuper optulerunt.

RG 29. 2. I forced the Parthians to give up to me the booty and the standards of three Roman armies and to beg as suppliants for the friendship of the Roman people.

Suet. *Div. Aug.* 21. 3. And the Parthians quickly yielded when Augustus claimed Armenia, and at his demand they returned the army-standards which they had taken from M. Crassus and M. Antonius. Moreover, they offered up hostages.

6a   6c

a RIC I², p. 62, no. 287. Denarius of Rome, *c.*19 BC. *Obv.* TVRPILI-ANVS III VIR, Head of Liber. *Rev.* CAESAR AVGVSTVS SIGN(*is*) RECE(*ptis*), Kneeling Parthian extending standard and vexillum.

b *RIC* I², p. 63, no. 306. Denarius of Rome, *c.*19 BC. *Obv.* L AQVIL-LIVS FLORVS III VIR, Bust of Virtus. *Rev.* CAESAR DIVI F(*ilius*) ARME(*nia*) CAPT(*a*), Kneeling Armenian, wearing tiara, extending both hands.

c *RIC* I², p. 50, no. 131. Aureus of (?)Spain, 18–17 BC. *Obv.* S P Q R IMP(*eratori*) CAESARI AVG(*usto*) COS XI TR(*ibunicia*) POT(*estate*) VI, Head of Augustus, bare. *Rev.* CIVIB(*us*) ET SIGN(*is*) MILIT(*aribus*) A PART(*his*) RECVP(*eratis*), Quadriga on triumphal arch flanked by soldiers.

The strength of Augustus' diplomatic and military pressure on the Parthians in 20 BC resulted in their restoration of Roman standards captured, in three earlier campaigns, from M. Crassus at Carrhae in 53 BC, from Decidius Saxa in 40 BC, and from Antony in 36 BC. Roman publicity after 20 BC suggests that Augustus' success was viewed less as a triumph of negotiation, however well backed militarily, than as an outright military victory (cf. Gagé, *RGDA*, on *RG* 29. 2 for literary references). The senate offered Augustus a triumph (Dio Cass. 54. 8 speaks of an ovation), but this he declined. Parthia had been Rome's traditional enemy for a long time (see Ziegler, *BRP*, reviewed by E. W. Gray in *JRS* 1965, pp. 269–71, and A. N. Sherwin-White, *RFPE*, pp. 322–41), and the return of the captured Roman standards not unnaturally became the most widely advertised of all aspects of foreign policy on the Augustan coinage. Celebratory coin-types were frequent at the mint of Rome, and also at the unidentified but prolific mints attributed to Spain in the strongly romanized west, where attention was called (CIVIB ET SIGN) not only to the recovery of the standards but also to the repatriation of Roman prisoners of war. Yet more celebratory types appeared *c.*19–18 BC at Pergamum (*RIC* I², pp. 82 f.) on Roman-weight gold and silver coins presumably struck for the payment of Augustus' back-up forces in the east. It might have been expected that Lugdunum—a mint with an essentially military focus—would also have alluded to the success against Parthia, for it was emphatic in its references to the earlier military victories in civil war at Naulochus (with the type of Diana) and Actium (with the type of Apollo) (*RIC* I², pp. 52 ff.); but the Lugdunum mint did not begin to issue imperial gold and silver coinage until *c.*15–13 BC, by which time the topicality of the Parthian success was fading. The unavailability of mints is responsible for the numismatic silence on certain other major events also, such as the closing of the temple of Janus in 29 and 25 BC (Dio Cass. 51. 20 and 53. 27), when the mint of Rome had not yet reopened, and the consecration of the Ara Pacis Augustae in 9 BC (*Fast. Praen.* under 30 January), when the mint of Rome had ceased to coin gold and silver (*RIC* I², pp. 73 ff.). It may be noted that Velleius (2. 91. 1) duly recorded the recovery of the Roman standards from Parthia. The credit for this he gave (2. 94. 4) to Tiberius, who earned his approval for other advances made under Augustus.

7. Augustus and the empty chariot

1. *RG* 4. 1. Bis ovans triumphavi et tris egi curulis triumphos.

2. Cassiodorus, *Chronica*, under 19 BC. Caesari ex provinciis redeunti currus cum corona aurea decretus est, quo ascendere noluit.

RG 4. 1. Twice I triumphed with an ovation, and three times I held curule triumphs.

Cassiodorus, *Chronica* (19 BC). When Caesar returned from the provinces he was decreed a chariot and a golden crown; but he would not ride in the chariot.

7a

a *RIC* I², p. 49, no. 119. Denarius of 'uncertain Spanish mint 2', *c.*18 BC. *Obv.* CAESARI AVGVSTO, Head of Augustus, laureate. *Rev.* S P Q R, Domed temple in which stands a *currus*, with shaft up, bearing legionary 'eagle' and four miniature galloping horses.

The three triumphs of Augustus were held on 13, 14, and 15 August in 29 BC, and celebrated his victories in Pannonia and related areas, at Actium, and (the climax) in Egypt (*Fast. Ant.* and *Barb.* under these dates; cf. Dio Cass. 51. 21). In 19 BC he returned to Rome from the east after imposing a settlement on Parthia, from which he had recovered the captured Roman standards (see no. 6). No actual hostilities against Parthia had taken place, and so no laurel could be ceremonially borne by Augustus as *triumphator* for presentation to Jupiter Capitolinus, according to the normal pattern of a triumph. Cassidorus' brief reference seems to indicate a substitute ceremony not explicitly recorded by historians of the time. Apparently a chariot was prepared by senatorial decree, and in this chariot Augustus was to ride (perhaps to the Capitol?) bearing a golden wreath. Two principal views have been taken of this decision. For Mommsen (*Res Gestae Divi Augusti* (ed. 2, Berlin, 1883), pp. 151 f.; *Römisches Staatsrecht* I (ed. 3, Leipzig, 1887), p. 395) it was a substitute ceremony offered because Augustus had refused a triumph, and for S. Weinstock (*DI*, pp. 273 f. with note 6) it was a privilege like that offered to Caesar—wheeled transport in Rome *in perpetuum*. Augustus, however, declined to ride in the chariot.

The 'uncertain Spanish mint 2' (*RIC* I², pp. 25 f.) produced a considerable series of aurei and denarii *c.*18 BC on which this event seems to be clearly commemorated. They show an empty *currus*, laid up in disuse with its shaft raised high, but containing a legionary 'eagle' and (equally symbolic of a triumph proper) four miniature galloping horses, all within the small, earlier temple of Mars Ultor (see no. 2), in which the standards recovered from Parthia were themselves deposited. Moreover, the head of Augustus on the obverse of these coins is shown laureate. It is therefore possible that something in the nature of a non-military triumph was organized to celebrate Augustus' successful pressure against Parthia, even though Augustus himself refused in the event to ride in procession, and that this was the ceremony referred to by Dio Cassius (54. 18) as an ovation. Although the imperial calendar made no reference to the occasion (cf. Gagé, *RGDA*, pp. 163 ff.), the coins of 'uncertain Spanish mint 2' are clear and emphatic: it is notable that the obverse legend is in the dative (*Caesari Augusto*), connecting the *currus* of the reverse as an honour conferred by the S P Q R upon Augustus. No reflection of this 'semi-triumph' of 19 BC is to be seen in the coinage of the mint of Rome, reopened *c.*19 BC (*RIC* I², pp. 61 ff.), although it gave wide publicity to the recovery of the standards. It would therefore be of considerable historical importance if we could identify 'uncertain Spanish mint 2' with certainty. Its coin-types declare an intimate imperial inspiration (*NACQT* 1983, pp. 151 ff.).

8. The *Ludi Saeculares* of 17 BC

1. *RG* 22. 2. Pro conlegio XV virorum magister conlegii collega M. Agrippa ludos saeclares C. Furnio C. Silano cos. feci.

2. Suet. *Div. Iul.* 88. Siquidem ludis, quos primos consecrato ei heres Augustus edebat, stella crinita per septem continuos dies fulsit exoriens circa undecimam horam, creditumque est animam esse Caesaris in caelum recepti; et hac de causa simulacro eius in vertice additur stella.

RG 22. 2. In the consulship of C. Furnius and C. Silanus, and on behalf of the college of the Fifteen, as head of that college and with M. Agrippa as my colleague I held the Secular Games.

Suet. *Div. Iul.* 88. At the games which his heir Augustus was holding for the first time to mark Caesar's consecration a comet shone for seven days on end, rising about the eleventh hour, and this was believed to be Caesar's soul taken into heaven. For this reason a star was added to his image.

8a   *8b*

a *RIC* I², p. 66, nos. 339 f. Aureus and denarius of Rome, *c.*17 BC. *Obv.* M SANQVINIVS III VIR, Youthful head with comet above.

Rev. AVGVST(*us*) DIVI F(*ilius*) LVDOS SAE(*culares*), Herald in long robe and feathered helmet holding winged caduceus and round shield on which is a six-pointed star.

b *RIC* I², p. 67, no. 350. Aureus of Rome, 16 BC. *Obv.* IMP CAESAR TR(*ibunicia*) POT(*estate*) IIX (= 16–15 BC), Head of Augustus, laureate. *Rev.* L MESCINIVS AVG(*ustus*) SVF(*fimenta*) P(*opulo dedit*), Augustus, wearing toga, seated on platform inscribed LVD(*i*) S(*aeculares*) giving *suffimenta* to one of two togate citizens.

c *RIC* I², p. 44, no. 37a. Denarius of 'uncertain Spanish mint 1', *c.*19–18 BC. *Obv.* CAESAR AVGVSTVS, Head of Augustus, oak-wreathed. *Rev.* DIVVS IVLIVS, Eight-rayed comet.

d *RIC* I², p. 85, nos. 539f. Aureus and denarius of uncertain mint, *c.*17 BC(?). *Obv.* CAESAR, Youthful head, oak-wreathed. *Rev.* AVGVST, Candelabrum ornamented with rams' heads, with crescent above, all within wreath entwined with bucrania and paterae.

Among the many public games held by Augustus (*RG* 22. 1 f.), the most solemn were the Secular Games of 17 BC, from 31 May to 3 June, the final day being marked by the performance of Horace's *Carmen Saeculare* on the Palatine and the Capitol (*CIL* vi. 32323). These games (for which see *saeculares* (*ludi*) in Pauly–Wissowa, *RE*; J. Gagé, *Recherches sur les jeux séculaires* (Paris, 1934); Brunt and Moore on *RG* 22. 2; Liebeschuetz, *CCRR*, pp. 97 f.; Weinstock, *DI*, pp. 370 ff., 376 ff., and esp. 379–82) were properly held every hundred years (cf. the διὰ ἑκατὸν ἐτῶν γεινομένας ... σαικλάρεις of the Greek text of the *RG*), but Augustus delayed them to (or preferred) the 110th year, just possibly (cf. Grant, *RAI*, p. 19) so as to include the decennial celebration of the constitutional settlement of 27 BC (see no. 4). Claudius' holding of the Secular Games in AD 47 (Tac. *Ann.* 11. 11) was intercalary and improper; Domitian's, in AD 88, was in the centennial reckoning from Augustus (Suet. *Dom.* 4. 3). Horace makes it clear that the Secular Games of Augustus were of a deeply religious and mystical character which went to the root of Roman national consciousness. And there were political changes in the air which might be thought to need religious sanction—the definitive settlement of 19 BC, the establishment of the dynastic principle, Agrippa with *tribunicia potestas* and *imperium* in 18 BC, and the adoption of C. and L. Caesar.

The Games were commemorated explicitly at the mint of Rome, reopened *c.*19 BC (*RIC* I², pp. 31 f., 61), by coins of the moneyers M. Sanquinius (*c.*17 BC) and L. Mescinius Rufus (16 BC). Sanquinius' coins showed a youthful head surmounted by a comet; and this *stella crinita*, henceforth associated with Divus Julius (as Suetonius records), was a type used by one of the two probable but unidentified mints of (?)Spain (*RIC* I², pp. 25 ff.). A mint conceivably situated in more eastern parts issued Augustan aurei and denarii which show, in their reverse type, what seem to be elements unmistakably appropriate to the Secular Games—candelabrum, bucrania and paterae (cf. *Class. Rev.* 1944, pp. 46 ff.): the crescent above the candelabrum could well allude to the nocturnal ceremonies when *Diana, lucidum caeli decus* (Horace, *Carm. Saec.* 1 f.) and *siderum regina bicornis . . . Luna* (*Carm. Saec.* 34 f.) held sway.

9. The mint of Lugdunum under Augustus and Tiberius

1. Strabo 4. 3. 2. αὐτὸ μὲν δὴ τὸ Λούγδουνον, ἐκτισμένον ὑπὸ λόφῳ κατὰ τὴν συμβολὴν τοῦ τε Ἄραρος τοῦ ποταμοῦ καὶ τοῦ Ῥοδανοῦ, κατέχουσι Ῥωμαῖοι. εὐανδρεῖ δὲ μάλιστα τῶν ἄλλων πλὴν Νάρβωνος· καὶ γὰρ ἐμπορίῳ χρῶνται καὶ τὸ νόμισμα χαράττουσιν ἐνταῦθα τό τε ἀργυροῦν καὶ τὸ χρυσοῦν οἱ τῶν Ῥωμαίων ἡγεμόνες. (Followed by a description of the Altar of Lugdunum in a temple at the confluence of the two rivers.)

Strabo 4. 3. 2. The Romans possess Lugdunum, founded below a ridge at the confluence of the Arar and the Rhône. It is the most populous of all the other cities [sc. in Gaul] except Narbo; for it is a centre of commerce, and the Roman emperors strike their silver and gold coinage there.

9b   9c

9d

a RIC I², p. 52, nos. 168f. Aureus and denarius of Lugdunum, *c.*15–13 BC. *Obv.* AVGVSTVS DIVI F(*ilius*), Head of Augustus, bare. *Rev.* IMP(*erator*) X, Butting bull.

b RIC I², p. 54, no. 192a. Aureus of Lugdunum, 11–10 BC. *Obv.* AVGVSTVS DIVI F, Head of Augustus, laureate. *Rev.* IMP XII, Apollo Citharoedus, ACT(*iacus*).

c RIC I², p. 56, nos. 219f. Aureus and denarius of Lugdunum, AD 13–14. *Obv.* CAESAR AVGVSTVS DIVI F PATER PATRIAE. Head of Augustus, laureate. *Rev.* PONTIF(*ex*) MAXIM(*us*), Female figure seated and holding sceptre and branch.

d RIC I², p. 57, no. 230. As of Lugdunum, 10 BC onwards. *Obv.* CAESAR PONT(*ifex*) MAX(*imus*), Head of Augustus, laureate. *Rev.* ROM(*ae*) ET AVG(*usti*), Front elevation of the Altar of Lugdunum decorated with the *corona civica* and flanked by male figures: Victories on columns above.

e RIC I², p. 95, nos. 25f. Aureus and denarius of Lugdunum, AD 14–37. *Obv.* TI(*berius*) CAESAR DIVI AVG(*usti*) F(*ilius*) AVGVSTVS, Head of Tiberius, laureate. *Rev.* As *c*.

Colonia Felix Munatia was founded at Lugdunum by L. Munatius Plancus in 43 BC (cf. Dio Cass. 46. 50. 3–5; Jullian, *HG*, pp. 42–93; A. Grenier in *Econ. Survey of Anc. Rome* iii, ed. T. Frank (Baltimore, 1937), esp. pp. 479–86; P. Wuilleumier, *Lyon, métropole des Gaules* (Paris, 1953); and M. Leglay in the *Princeton Encyclopedia of Classical Sites*). A small foundation-issue of *aes* coins was produced there, followed not long afterwards by a more extensive *aes* issue in the name of Octavian with Divus Julius (Grant, *FITA*, pp. 206f.). The Lugdunum mint may have continued to strike colonial *aes* coins even later. A mint, and the relevant expertise of operating it, were now in any case established there; and it is probable that this mint was responsible for the production of the very common 'first Altar of Lyons' asses (with some much less common sestertii) struck for Augustus after the dedication of the Altar of Rome and Augustus in 10 BC (Suet. *Div. Claud.* 2. 1; on the cult see J. Deininger, *Die Provinziallandtage der römischen Kaiserzeit* (Munich, 1965), and A. J. Christopherson in *Historia* 1968, pp. 351–66), by which time he was *pontifex maximus*: an even larger (and mainly dated) 'second Altar' *aes* series was to follow *c.*AD 9–14 (*RIC* I², pp. 57 f., nos. 231–48). It is possible that the abundant 'first Altar' issue was produced in part at mints in Gaul adjacent to Lugdunum (cf. J.-B. Giard in *Rev. Num.* 1967, pp. 119 ff.); but the fact of central importance is that a mint at Lugdunum was striking *aes* coins in and after 43 BC, from 10 BC, and from AD 9. No direct evidence exists to prove that Augustus extended the minting activity of Lugdunum from regional *aes* to more widely circulating imperial aurei and denarii. But the chain of argument is strong. Strabo, writing under Tiberius, and emphasizing the population and the commercial activity of Lugdunum at the confluence of the Saône and the Rhône, stated specifically that the Roman ἡγεμόνες (most probably 'emperors', less probably 'governors', though these would have been under imperial orders) struck at Lugdunum τὸ νόμισμα of silver and gold, i.e. their (collective) coinage of aurei and denarii (cf. my review in *Num. Chron.* 1952, pp. 139 ff., of H. R. W. Smith, *Problems Historical and Numismatic in the Reign of Augustus*). Strabo did not state that they there struck νόμισμα, *some* coinage of silver and gold.

Tiberius' long series of aurei and denarii (nearly all of it undated, but showing clear internal signs of time-sequence) is therefore to be attributed to the mint of Lugdunum. It is distinguished by the repeated use of the PONTIF MAXIM reverse type (see *e*). This had first appeared under Augustus in AD 13–14 (see *c*). Moreover the portrait-treatment and the general technique of Tiberius' gold and silver is the same as that of Augustus, and Tiberius' portrait under Augustus (*RIC* I², p. 56, no. 226) is closely paralleled by his portrait after accession (*RIC* I², p. 95, no. 23). Finally, we should note that the portraiture of Augustus, after the 'laureate head' style was adopted for his gold and silver from 11–10 BC (see *b*), was based quite clearly on the model used for the 'first Altar' *aes* from 10 BC (see *d*). From all this it appears to be virtually certain that Augustus used the mint of Lugdunum (presumably expanded and elaborated) for the production of aurei and denarii from *c.*11 BC—possibly even from *c.*15 BC (see *a*; butting bull = the Rhône?)—and continued its use thereafter throughout his principate (*RIC* I², pp. 53 ff., nos. 186–226), and that Tiberius continued this arrangement. There was much to recommend it. Lugdunum lay at a comparatively short distance from the Rhine, the line of communication which linked a string of troop concentrations against Germany, and therefore facilitated regular payments to those troops: it has been remarked (cf. K. Hopkins in *JRS* 1980, p. 101) that there was a distinction between an outer ring of frontier provinces containing the armies and an inner ring of tax-exporting provinces. Rome, it should be observed, ceased to coin aurei and denarii just when Lugdunum was beginning to do so. In addition, Lugdunum occupied a position conveniently available for the transport of uncoined bullion from the mines of Spain. To initiate minting of gold and silver at Lugdunum would have involved the amassing of bullion in considerable quantity, and it has been suggested in this connection (by Mattingly in *BMCRE* I, p. cxiii) that Dio Cassius (54. 21) misconstrued the seemingly rapacious activities of Licinus, procurator in Gaul, in 15 BC. As a primary precious-metal mint thereafter Lugdunum would have required special protection: Tiberius had a mint-official there, and an urban cohort was stationed there at some time early in the principate (*CIL* xiii, 1820, 1499; the posting of the cohort is dated to 16–13 BC by Dreis, *CU*, pp. 28–31).

10. Augustus' dynastic plans

1. *RG* 14. 1 f. Filios meos, quos iuvenes mihi eripuit fortuna, Gaium et Lucium Caesares honoris mei caussa senatus populusque Romanus annum quintum et decimum agentis consules designavit ut eum magistratum inirent post quinquennium. Et ex eo die quo deducti sunt in forum, ut interessent consiliis publicis decrevit

senatus. Equites autem Romani universi principem iuventutis utrumque eorum parmis et hastis argenteis donatum appellaverunt.

2. Tac. *Ann.* 1. 3. Ceterum Augustus subsidia dominationi Claudium Marcellum sororis filium admodum adulescentem pontificatu et curuli aedilitate, M. Agrippam, ignobilem loco, bonum militia et victoriae socium geminatis consulatibus extulit, mox, defuncto Marcello, generum sumpsit; Tiberium Neronem et Claudium Drusum privignos imperatoriis nominibus auxit, integra etiam tum domo sua. Nam genitos Agrippa Gaium ac Lucium in familiam Caesarum induxerat, necdum posita puerili praetexta principes iuventutis appellari, destinari consules specie recusantis flagrantissime cupiverat. Ut Agrippa vita concessit, Lucium Caesarem euntem ad Hispaniensis exercitus, Gaium remeantem Armenia et vulnere invalidum mors fato propera vel novercae Liviae dolus abstulit, Drusoque pridem extincto Nero solus e privignis erat, illuc cuncta vergere: filius, collega imperii, consors tribuniciae potestatis adsumitur, omnisque per exercitus ostentatur.

3. Suet. Tib. 23. Inlatum deinde Augusti testamentum ... recitavit (Tiberius) per libertum. Testamenti initium fuit: quoniam atrox fortuna Gaium et Lucium filios mihi eripuit, Tiberius Caesar mihi ex parte dimidia et sextante heres esto.

RG 14. 1 f. My sons Gaius and Lucius Caesar, whom fate snatched from me, were each in their fifteenth year when the senate and people of Rome, in honour to me, designated them five years in advance as consuls. And the senate decreed that they should participate in public business from the day on which they were formally introduced into the forum. The Roman knights, for their part, were unanimous in entitling them Princes of the Youth, and gave each of them a silver shield and spear.

Tac. *Ann.* 1. 3. Now Augustus provided himself with certain props for his political mastery. Claudius Marcellus, his sister's son, and quite young, was made a priest and a curule aedile. Marcus Agrippa, of undistinguished birth, but a fine soldier, and his comrade in victory, was made consul twice running, and presently became Augustus' son-in-law upon the death of Marcellus. Tiberius Nero and Claudius Drusus, Augustus' stepsons, were honoured with the style 'imperator'. At this time Augustus' own family was still intact. For he had admitted into it Agrippa's sons Gaius and Lucius, and before they had even laid aside the 'junior toga' he had conceived the most urgent desire (whatever his show of outward reluctance) to have them named 'Princes of the Youth' and designated as consuls in advance. But Agrippa died; a premature fate (or the wiles of their stepmother Livia) removed Lucius Caesar as he journeyed to the armies of Spain, and Gaius as he returned, wounded and weak, from Armenia; Drusus was long dead. So Nero alone remained of the step-children, and he became the focus of everything. He was taken up as adopted son, colleague in military command, and partner in tribunician power, and was paraded throughout the armies.

Suet. *Tib.* 23. Augustus' will was then brought in, and Tiberius had it read by a freedman. It began with the words: 'Since savage ill-fortune has snatched my sons Gaius and Lucius away from me, let Tiberius Caesar be my heir as to two-thirds of my property.'

10b   *10c*   *10e*

a Grant, *FITA*, p. 81. Bronze sestertius(?) of Augustus, 25 BC; mint of Byzacene in Africa(?). *Obv.* IMP(*erator*) CAESAR DIVI F(*ilius*) AVGVST(*us*) COS IX, Head of Augustus crowned by Victory. *Rev.* M(*arcus*) ACILIVS GLABRIO PRO COS (*proconsul*), Young male and female heads confronted.

b *RIC* I², p. 51, nos. 155–8. Bronze asses(?) of the mint of Nemausus (Nîmes) in Gaul, *c.*20 BC–AD 10. *Obv.* IMP DIVI F, Heads of Agrippa and Augustus back to back. *Rev.* COL(*onia*) NEM(*ausus*): sometimes NIM. Wreathed palm-shoot behind chained crocodile.

c *RIC* I², p. 55, nos. 206f. Aurei and denarii of Lugdunum, 2 BC–AD 4 or beyond. *Obv.* CAESAR AVGVSTVS DIVI F(*ilius*) PATER PATRIAE, Head of Augustus, laureate. *Rev.* C(*aius*)

L(*ucius*) CAESARES AVGVSTI F(*ilii*) COS (*consules*) DESIG(*nati*) PRINC(*ipes*) IVVENT(*utis*), Gaius and Lucius, each in toga, standing facing, each resting hand on shield; spear behind each shield; above, priestly simpulum and lituus.

d *RIC* I², p. 73, no. 406. Denarius of Rome, 13 BC. *Obv.* CAESAR AVGVSTVS, Head of Augustus, bare. *Rev.* C(*aius*) SVLPIC(*ius*) PLATORIN(*us*), Augustus and Agrippa, bareheaded and togate, seated on *bisellium* on rostral platform; upright staff or spear on left.

e *RIC* I², p. 78, no. 469. Bronze as of Rome, AD 10–11. *Obv.* TI(*berius*) CAESAR AVGVST(*i*) F(*ilius*) IMPERAT(*or*) V, Head of Tiberius, bare. *Rev.* PONTIFEX TRIBVN(*icia*) POTESTATE XII around S(*enatus*) C(*onsulto*).

f *RIC* I², p. 56, nos. 225f. Aurei and denarii of Lugdunum, AD 13–14. *Obv.* CAESAR AVGVSTVS DIVI F(*ilius*) PATER PATRIAE, Head of Augustus, laureate. *Rev.* TI(*berius*) CAESAR AVG(*usti*) F(*ilius*) TR(*ibunicia*) POT(*estate*) XV, Head of Tiberius, bare.

The young Marcellus, nephew of Augustus, and married to his daughter Julia, was the first in the tormented series of machinations by which Augustus clearly sought to project his own power into a future dynasty (see R. Syme, *RR*, pp. 331–48); and high hopes were reposed upon him (cf. Vergil, *Aen.* 6. 868 ff.), though these are reflected only dimly, and in any case not certainly, on a provincial *aes* coin (see *a*) which may commemorate his marriage in 25 BC. Two years later he was dead (cf. A. J. Woodman on Vell. Pat. 2. 93. 1; and Plut. *Marcellus* 30): the mint of Rome, which might otherwise have advertised his prospects, had not yet been reopened (*RIC* I², pp. 31 f.). The widowed Julia was now married off to Agrippa, of whom Maecenas said, according to Dio Cassius (54. 6. 5), that Augustus must either make him his son-in-law or destroy him (on Agrippa's position at this point see Reinhold, *Agrippa*, p. 97). Agrippa, indeed, had been Augustus' master strategist and chief coadjutor in the civil war, and it was as such that his portrait, wearing a combined rostral crown (adorned with the 'beaks' of ships captured at Actium and elsewhere) and laurel-wreath, shared with that of Augustus the obverse of the great *aes* series of coins struck at Nemausus from *c.*20 BC onwards (see *b*), the reverse of which showed the civic badge of a captive crocodile and a wreathed palm-shoot, apparently because Nemausus received a settlement of men involved in the capture of Egypt (see Grant, *SMACA*, p. 120).

Julia bore two sons to Agrippa, Gaius in 20 BC (Dio Cass. 54. 8) and Lucius in 17 BC (Dio Cass. 54. 18), in which latter year Augustus adopted them as sons and Caesars. In 18 BC Agrippa became colleague with Augustus in the *tribunicia potestas* (he was tr. pot. VI at his death in 12 BC; cf. *E. and J.*[2] 71), and his position was perhaps enhanced in 17 if it was in that year (and see here the contrary view of M. Reinhold, *Marcus Agrippa*, p. 104 n. 28) that he was selected by Augustus to be one of the *magistri collegii quindecimvirorum* in charge of the Ludi Saeculares (*RG* 22. 2; see no. 8 above). His prominence by 13 BC is evident in the coinage of Rome in that year (see *d*). Tiberius, one of the two consuls of 13 (*E. and J.*[2] p. 37), was presumably regarded as being next in the line of succession (for discussion of his position see Seager, *Tiberius*, pp. 18–47, and Levick, *TP*, chs. iii–iv). But the scheme was radically changed when Agrippa died in 12. Although Tiberius had received a five-year grant of *tribunicia potestas*, he retired to Rhodes in 6 BC, the year in which Rome witnessed public pressure for Gaius Caesar to be made consul (Dio Cass. 55. 9. 2); and in 5 BC, with whatever outward show of reluctance, Augustus declared his hand. Gaius was to be designated consul for AD 1, and Lucius for AD 4: meanwhile they were to be styled *principes inventutis*, and Gaius became a *pontifex*, Lucius an *augur*.

Augustus might now consider his dynasty secure, and a huge issue of gold and silver coins (see *c*), including splendid gold multiples (*RIC* I[2], p. 55, no. 204), poured out from the mint of Lugdunum to celebrate his new plan, and possibly also (Grant, *RAI*, pp. 22 ff.) to mark the 25th anniversary of the settlement of 27 BC. Many civic issues of coinage throughout the empire commemorated the dawn of the new dynasty. But *atrox fortuna*—Augustus' own words (see B. Levick in *Class. Rev.* 1972, pp. 309–11)—brought the death of Lucius in AD 2 (before he could become consul) and of Gaius in AD 4. The Julian succession (even if it might have involved some kind of dual principate) was extinct. Augustus, now ageing, was left with only one 'subsidium dominationi', Tiberius, whom he at once adopted as his son (*Fast. Amit.* under 26 or 27 June; cf. Vell.

Pat. 2. 103 and Syme, *RR*, pp. 419–39). And Tiberius' military experience was unrivalled. Before his retirement to Rhodes he had reduced Illyricum to provincial order and military security, and had advanced the Roman position on the east bank of the Rhine. After AD 4, now returned from Rhodes, he first put down the Pannonian revolt and later preserved the Rhine frontier after the *clades Variana* of AD 9. Nevertheless, he received no publicity of any kind on the imperial coinage until AD 10–11, and then only (see *e*) on the *aes* of Rome (gold and silver of the mint of Rome having now ceased; cf. *RIC* I², p. 34). Lugdunum followed with conspicuous issues for Tiberius in AD 13–14 (see *f*), including some (*RIC* I², p. 56, nos. 221–4) celebrating his military triumphs. Six years had passed since his adoption as Augustus' son, and we might well accuse Augustus of a reluctance to publicize Tiberius if there were not some reason (cf. Suet. *Tib.* 15 ff.) to suppose that Tiberius himself deprecated undue military recognition at this period in the face of Augustus' desire to enhance his obvious *maiestas*.

11. Augustus' state benefactions

1. *RG* 17. Quater pecunia mea iuvi aerarium, ita ut sestertium milliens et quingentiens ad eos qui praerant (*sic*) aerario detulerim. Et M. Lepido et L. Arruntio consulibus in aerarium militare quod ex consilio meo constitutum est, ex quo praemia darentur militibus qui vicena aut plura stipendia emeruissent, sestertium milliens et septingentiens ex patrimonio meo detuli.

2. Suet. *Div. Aug.* 30. Quo autem facilius undique urbs adiretur, desumpta sibi Flaminia via Arimino tenus munienda reliquas triumphalibus viris ex manubiali pecunia sternendas distribuit.

3. Suet. *Div. Aug.* 41. Liberalitatem omnibus ordinibus per occasiones frequenter exhibuit. Nam et invecta urbi Alexandrino triumpho regia gaza tantam copiam nummariae rei effecit ut faenore deminuto plurimum agrorum pretiis accesserit . . . Congiaria populo frequenter dedit . . . Frumentum quoque in annonae difficultatibus saepe levissimo, interdum nullo pretio, viritim admensus est.

RG 17. Four times I assisted the public treasury with my own money, depositing 150 million sesterces in all to those in charge of that treasury. And in the consulship of M. Lepidus and L. Arruntius I deposited 170 million sesterces, from my inherited fortune, in the military treasury which was set up on my advice for the payment of rewards to those soldiers with 20 years of service, or more, to their credit.

Suet. *Div. Aug.* 30. And so that the approaches to Rome could be made easier from all directions, he personally defrayed repair-work on the Flaminian Way as far as Ariminum and assigned the rest of the roads to men who, having celebrated triumphs, should pave them from out of their spoils of war.

Suet. *Div. Aug.* 41. He frequently showed liberality to all classes as occasion arose. For example, when the royal [i.e. Egyptian] treasure was borne into Rome in his Alexandrian triumph he was able to produce so much coinage that interest rates dropped and land-values rose sharply . . . He often gave public largesse . . . and when the corn-supply was running low he made individual gifts of grain, often at a very low cost, sometimes at no cost at all.

11a   **11b**

a *RIC* I², p. 68, no. 360. Denarius of Rome, 16 BC. *Obv.* AVGVSTVS TR(*ibunicia*) POT(*estate*) VII (July 17 BC–June 16 BC), Head of Augustus, bare. *Rev.* L VINICIVS L(*ucii*) F(*ilius*) III VIR, Cippus inscribed S P Q R / IMP(*eratori*) CAE(*sari*) / QVOD V(*iae*) M(*unitae*) S(*unt*) EX / EA P(*ecunia*) Q(*uam*) IS / AD A(*erarium*) DE(*tulit*).

b *RIC* I², p. 50, no. 140. Aureus of 'uncertain Spanish mint 2', *c.*18–16 BC. *Obv.* S P Q R IMP(*eratori*) CAESARI, Head of Augustus, bare. *Rev.* QVOD VIAE MVN(*itae*) SVNT, Augustus, crowned by Victory, in elephant-biga on double arch on viaduct.

c *RIC* I², p. 50, no. 142. Denarius of 'uncertain Spanish mint 2', *c*.18–16 BC. *Obv.* S P Q R IMP(*eratori*) CAESARI, Head of Augustus, bare. *Rev.* QVOD / VIAE / MVN(*itae*) / SVNT in four lines between two arches on viaduct, each bearing equestrian statue and trophy.

Appendix 1 of the *RG* (written, like Appendix 2, in the third person) states that the money given personally by Augustus to the *aerarium*, to the *plebs* of Rome, and to time-expired soldiers, amounted to 600 million denarii, equal to 2,400 million sesterces, the accounting denomination used in all cases but two (*RG* 15. 2 and 4) by Augustus himself. This was an average of over 13 million denarii (52 million sesterces) for every year of his reign from 31 BC. In some cases the object of his generosity is specified, as with the 170 million sesterces (42½ million denarii) given to establish the *aerarium militare* in AD 6 (Dio Cass. 55. 23 and 26)—a fund, afterwards supported by the 5% inheritance tax and the 1% sales tax (cf. Suet. *Div. Aug.* 42. 2) from which army veterans could be paid a bounty on retirement. In other cases, benefactions are known, but not their individual amounts. The four occasions of help to the *aerarium Saturni* totalled 150 million sesterces (37½ million denarii) and appear to have made possible the repair or construction of roads both in Italy, as Suetonius recorded (cf. also *CIL* xi. 365 and Dio Cass. 53. 22), and in Spain, if the attribution of 'uncertain Spanish mint 2' to a Spanish province (*RIC* I², pp. 25f.) is correct. Italian road-work is dated to 27 BC (*cos. sept.*) and 17–16 BC (the *tr. pot. VII* of the coins): coins again date the (?)Spanish road-work to *c*.17 BC.

Suetonius, in *Div. Aug.* 30, clearly implies that Augustus' expenditure on the Via Flaminia (on which see *E. and J.*² no. 286 = *ILS* 84) in 27 BC came from his spoils of war. And, as he records in *Div. Aug.* 41, it was from the spoils of war—and specifically from the captured royal treasure of Egypt—that he was able to coin so much new money that interest rates fell (cf. E. Lo Cascio in *JRS* 1981, pp. 85f.) and land-values rose. No even approximate estimate of the monetary worth of Augustus' *manubiae* after 31 BC has come down to us. All that is evident is that he became the possessor of wealth which, even if not supreme (Lucan 3. 168), was at any rate comparable with that of the state itself. It enabled him to repair roads, subsidize the *aerarium Saturni*, establish the *aerarium militare*, distribute *congiaria* and *frumentationes* (*RG* 15; cf. Dio Cass. 51. 21 and 53. 28 for the *congiaria* of 29 and 24 BC, the latter *ex patrimonio* but obviously facilitated by the *manubiae*, and note that Augustus' acceptance of the *cura annonae*, *RG* 5. 2, resulted in no fewer than twelve *frumentationes* in 23 BC. For general discussion of his *liberalitates* see Millar, *ERW*, pp. 189–201; Z. Yavetz, *Plebs and Princeps* (Oxford, 1969), p. 133; Rogers, *SRT*, pp. 3–22. For the *aerarium militare* see Campbell, *ERA*, pp. 172 f., and for *frumentationes* Rickman, *CSAR*, p. 186, and Van Berchem, *DBA*). He could also afford to construct and repair buildings (*RG* 19–21) and to stage a series of notable games, including the Ludi Saeculares (see no. **8** above). This vast record of benefactions to the state resulted in a natural blurring of the distinction between the *aerarium*, the state treasury, on the one hand, and the emperor's *res privata*, or privy purse, on the other (cf. *AJPhil.* 1945, pp. 151 ff.; A. H. M. Jones, *JRS* 1950, pp. 22–9, and P. A. Brunt, *JRS* 1966, pp. 75–91).

12. The imperial coinage
as a universal currency

1. Epictetus, *Dissert.* 3. 3. 3. τὸ τοῦ Καίσαρος νόμισμα οὐκ ἔξεστιν ἀποδοκιμάσαι τῷ τραπεζίτῃ οὐδὲ τῷ λαχανοπώλῃ, ἀλλ᾽ ἂν δείξῃς, θέλει οὐ θέλει, προέσθαι αὐτὸν δεῖ τὸ ἀντ᾽ αὐτοῦ πωλούμενον.

2. Dio Cass. 64. 6. 1. τό τε γὰρ ἐπὶ Νέρωνος καὶ τὸ ἐπὶ Γάλβου τοῦ τε Ὄθωνος κοπὲν νόμισμα ἐτήρησεν (sc. Vitellius) οὐκ ἀγανακτῶν ταῖς εἰκόσιν αὐτῶν.

3. Tac. *Ann.* 4. 37. Cum divus Augustus sibi atque urbi Romae templum apud Pergamum sisti non prohibuisset, qui omnia facta dictaque eius vice legis observem, . . . exemplum . . . secutus sum.

Epictetus, *Dissert.* 3. 3. 3. Neither banker nor greengrocer is allowed to reject the imperial coinage. If you show it to them, then, like it or not, they must produce the corresponding merchandise in exchange.

Dio Cass. 64. 6. 1. Vitellius retained the coinages struck for Nero, Galba, and Otho, having no objection to their portraits on them.

Tac. *Ann.* 4. 37. Augustus did not forbid the erection of a temple at Pergamum in honour of himself and of Rome, and so I, who treat all his deeds and utterances as law, have followed his example.

a *RIC* I², p. 82, no. 505. Silver cistophorus (= 3 denarii) of Pergamum, 19 BC. *Obv.* IMP(*erator*) IX TR(*ibunicia*) PO(*testate*) V, Head of Augustus, bare. *Rev.* COM(*mune*) ASIAE, Temple inscribed ROM(*ae*) ET AVGVST(*o*).

b *RIC* I², p. 80, no. 479. Silver cistophorus (= 3 denarii) of Ephesus, c.(?)25 BC. *Obv.* IMP(*erator*) CAESAR, Head of Augustus, bare. *Rev.* AVGVSTVS, Garlanded altar sculpted with two confronting hinds.

c *RIC* I², p. 100, no. 86. Silver drachma of Caesarea in Cappadocia, AD 33–4. *Obv.* TI(*berius*) CAES(*ar*) AVG(*ustus*) P(*ontifex*) M(*aximus*) R(*ibunicia*) P(*otestate*) XXXV, Head of Tiberius, laureate. *Rev.* DRVSVS CAES(*ar*) TI(*berii*) AVG(*usti*) F(*ilius*) COS II R(*ibunicia*) P(*otestate*) IT(*erum*), Head of Drusus, bare.

Aurei and denarii of the imperial coinage, issued at whichever of the imperial mints, were obligatory legal tender, and thus universally acceptable, throughout the Roman empire, east as well as west (see the chart of K. Hopkins in *JRS* 1980, p. 113, fig. 4), at the fixed rate (Dio Cass. 55. 12) of 25 denarii to the

aureus. A *princeps* had no objection to the continuing circulation of the precious metals of his predecessors (the base denarii
of M. Antonius were still in currency in the third century: see,
for example, Sutherland, *CCRB*, pp. 37 f.), and the recall of
former issues—through bankers, moneychangers, and the
aerarium itself—would be attempted only if there were a
notable downward change in the weight-standard or fineness
of the coinage, as under Nero (see no. 38 below). Even if such
recall was from time to time attempted, much of any preceding
coinage of superior weight or fineness would quite certainly
have been immobilized by hoarding, or demonetized by melting down. The report (Dio Cass. 50. 22; see no. 32 below) that
demonetization of the *aes* coinage of Gaius was among the
early acts of Claudius (Suet. *Div. Claud.* 11) is difficult to accept
on economic and other grounds.

The universality of the aureus was total: the only other gold
coins in production within the imperial world—and they were
few by comparison—were those of the dependent kings of
Bosporus (*BMC Pontus . . .*, pp. 48 ff.). Silver denarii, however,
were not always popular in the east, which from Greek times
onwards had often preferred larger silver units. Recognizing
this fact, Augustus established two prolific eastern mints to
coin large 3-denarius 'cistophori'. Both were in the province of
Asia, one quite certainly at Pergamum (compare passage 3
with coin *a*) and one almost equally certainly at Ephesus,
marked (see *b*) by the altar and hinds of the temple of Diana.
These mints, which continued to work, on and off, for a
century and more (cf. Sutherland, *CA*, *passim*), produced a
very large and economically significant coinage under Augustus (cf. Magie, *RRAM*, p. 442). Each struck three reverse types
simultaneously (as multiple obverse die-links conclusively
show), and each was thus presumably organized on a three-
officina basis comparable to that obtaining under Augustus at
Rome itself with the *tresviri monetales* (see no. 13). This 'cistophoric' coinage of Augustus remained substantially in circulation until Hadrian's great cistophoric recoinage (cf.
H. Herzfelder, *Num. Chron.* 1936, pp. 1 ff.), attesting a
currency-life of well over a century for these large-sized eastern
silver issues.

13. The *tresviri monetales* at Rome under Augustus

1. Dio Cass. 54. 26. 6. οἱ δὲ δὴ εἴκοσιν οὗτοι ἄνδρες ἐκ τῶν ἓξ καὶ εἴκοσίν εἰσιν, οἵ τε τρεῖς οἱ τὰς τοῦ θανάτου δίκας προστεταγμένοι, καὶ οἱ ἕτεροι τρεῖς οἱ τὸ τοῦ νομίσματος κόμμα μεταχειριζόμενοι, οἵ τε τέσσαρες οἱ τῶν ἐν τῷ ἄστει ὁδῶν ἐπιμελούμενοι, καὶ οἱ δέκα οἱ ἐπὶ τῶν δικαστηρίων τῶν ἐς τοὺς ἑκατὸν ἄνδρας κληρουμένων ἀποδεικνύμενοι (of 13 BC).

Dio Cass. 54. 26. 6. These twenty men are part of the body of twenty-six—the three in charge of capital sentences, the three others conducting the striking of coinage, the four taking care of the roads in Rome, and the ten appointed for the hearing of the civil court-cases.

13a

13b

a RIC I², pp. 75 f., nos. 426, 429, and 433. Dupondii(?) of Rome, *c.*7 BC. *Obv.* CAESAR AVGVST(*us*) PONT(*ifex*) MAX(*imus*) TRIBVNIC(*ia*) POT(*estate*), Victory crowning Augustus' head with laurel. *Rev.* P LVRIVS AGRIPPA (or M SALVIVS OTHO or M MAECILIVS TVLLVS) III VIR A A A F F around S C.

b RIC I², pp. 76 f., no. 443. Quadrans of Rome, *c.*5 BC. *Obv.* APRONIVS MESSALLA III VIR around altar. *Rev.* GALVS SISENNA A A A F F around S C.

Under the republic the annually appointed *collegia* of the *tresviri aere argento auro flando feriundo* (the historical order in which the three coinage-metals were successively melted, refined, and struck) had lasted, with the occasional addition of extra members for special purposes, as part of the vigintivirate (with duties as defined by Dio Cassius) until Julius Caesar changed the number of moneyers to four (see no. 1 above). The *vigintiviri*, ranking as junior magistrates, were generally but not always (see *E. and J.*[2] no. 235) aspirants to senatorial rank. When Augustus reopened the mint of Rome for a regular series of coinage, probably *c.*19 BC (cf. *RIC* I², pp. 31 ff.), he reverted to the pre-Caesarian number of three *monetales*: this is most clearly evident from the dated coinage (16 BC) of the three moneyers L. Mescinius Rufus, L. Vinicius, and C. Antistius Vetus (*RIC* I², pp. 67 ff.), and from the three moneyers' names on the exactly matching *aes* coins of *c.*7 BC (see *a*), in which Mattingly saw a reflection of Tiberius' triumphant campaigns against Dalmatians, Pannonians, and Germans from 12 BC onwards (Mattingly, *BMCRE* I, p. xcviii; cf. Suet. *Tib.* 9). Not all moneyers coined in all metals (cf. *RIC* I², pp. 61 ff.): presumably each *collegium* of moneyers was instructed by the praetors (who from 23 BC controlled the *aerarium*: see no. 14 below) to strike what in any year was actually or provisionally required by way of new coinage. Dio Cassius' account of the εἴκοσι, the vigintivirate, suggests that the change to the number of three moneyers came in 13 BC, but, as has been shown above, three were at work in 16 BC, and it is not difficult to detect three from *c.*19 BC. However, change at the mint of Rome is evident after 12 BC, when it ceased to produce gold and silver (Lugdunum by then being in regular production: see no. 9 above). Moreover, when—for reasons now only to be conjectured—the production of *aes* quadrantes, first begun by the *monetales c.*9–8 BC, rose to a peak *c.*5–4 BC (see *b*), the coins themselves show quite certainly that they were issued by *quattuorviri* and not by *tresviri*. After *c.*4 BC no coinage can be assigned to the mint of Rome until AD 10 (*RIC* I², p. 78). *Aes* coinage was then resumed, but the coins now no longer bore moneyers' names. The office of *tresvir a. a. a. f. f.* nevertheless continued for a further two and a half centuries, as epigraphic evidence shows, and carried a certain prestige (cf. D. McAlindon in *JRS* 1957, pp. 191–5, and R. J. A. Talbert, *The Senate of Imperial Rome* (Princeton, 1984), p. 63).

14. The formula *S C* on Augustus' *aes* coinage

1. Tac. *Ann.* 13. 29. Varie habita ac saepe mutata eius rei (i.e. the cura tabularum publicarum) forma. Nam Augustus senatui permisit deligere praefectos; deinde ambitu suffragiorum suspecto, sorte ducebantur ex numero praetorum qui praeessent. Neque id diu mansit, quia sors deerrabat ad parum idoneos. Tunc Claudius quaestores rursum imposuit iisque, ne metu offensionum segnius consulerent, extra ordinem honores promisit: sed deerat robur aetatis eum primum magistratum capessentibus. Igitur Nero praetura perfunctos et experientia probatos delegit (of AD 56).

2. Tac. *Ann.* 5. 8. Relatum inde de P. Vitellio et Pomponio Secundo. Illum indices arguebant claustra aerarii, cui praefectus erat, et militarem pecuniam rebus novis obtulisse (of AD 31).

Tac. *Ann.* 13. 29. The system (i.e. of the financial office) had undergone frequent change. Augustus allowed the senate to choose *praefecti*, and then, when corrupt voting was suspected, lots were drawn from among the praetors. That plan did not last long, as lottery lighted on men who were not well enough qualified. Claudius then restored quaestors to the job, and promised them special promotion lest they might be too slack in their duties through fear of giving offence. But since they were men now holding their first public magistracy, they lacked maturity; and Nero therefore chose ex-praetors, proved by experience.

Tac. *Ann.* 5. 8. The cases of P. Vitellius and Pomponius Secundus then came up. The former was charged by his accusers with having offered the keys of the public treasury (of which he was *praefectus*) in aid of revolution, together with the military treasury.

14a

14c   *14e*

a *RIC* I², p. 65, no. 327. Sestertius of Rome, *c.*18 BC. *Obv.* OB CIVIS SERVATOS, Oak-wreath flanked by two laurel-branches. *Rev.* TI(*tus*) QVINCTIVS CRISPIN(*us*) SVLPIC(*ianus*) III VIR A A A F F around S C.

b *RIC* I², p. 65, no. 326. Dupondius of Rome, *c.*18 BC. *Obv.* AVGVSTVS TRIBVNIC(*ia*) POTEST(*ate*) in oak-wreath. *Rev.* C CENSORINVS L(*ucii*) F(*ilius*) AVG(*uris*) III VIR A A A F F around S C.

c *RIC* I², p. 70, no. 379. As of Rome, 16 BC. *Obv.* CAESAR AVGVSTVS TRIBVNIC(*ia*) POTEST(*ate*), Head of Augustus, bare. *Rev.* C GALLIVS LVPERCVS III VIR A A A F F around S C.

d *RIC* I², p. 74, no. 422. Quadrans of Rome, *c.*9 BC. *Obv.* LAMIA SILIVS ANNIVS, S C, Cornucopia. *Rev.* III VIR A A A F F around garlanded altar.

e *RIC* I², p. 68, no. 358. Denarius of Rome, 16 BC. *Obv.* I(*ovi*) O(*ptimo*) M(*aximo*) S(*enatus*) P(*opulus*)Q(*ue*) R(*omanus*) V(*otis*) S(*olutis*) PR(*o*) S(*alute*) IMP(*eratoris*) CAE(*saris*) QVOD PER EV(*m*) R(*es*) P(*ublica*) IN AMP(*liore*) ATQ(*ue*) TRA*N*(*quilliore*) S(*tatu*) E(*st*) in oak-wreath (see no. 4 above). *Rev.* L MESCINIVS RVFVS III VIR, S C, Cippus inscribed IMP(*erator*, or -*ori*) CAES(*ar*, -*ari*) AVGV(*stus*, -*sto*) COMM(*uni*) CONS(*ensu*).

Under the republic certain issues of denarii had been struck at Rome bearing exceptional formulae, such as EX A(*rgento*)

P(*ublico*), EX S(*enatus*) C(*onsulto*), S C, S C D(*e*) T(*hesauro*), indicating that the moneyers concerned (not normally members of the annual *collegium* of the *tresviri a. a. a. f. f.*; see no. 13 above) were specially appointed to coin silver allocated by the senate for special purposes. The normal republican *tresviri* coined the quota of silver which was allocated to them, it is to be presumed, by the quaestors, in whose charge the *aerarium* lay. Under Augustus a few aurei and denarii of Rome bore the formula S C or EX S C, but it is at once obvious that in such cases the formula refers narrowly to the coin-type: that of Mescinius Rufus, for example (*e*), shows a cippus honouring Augustus *senatus consulto*, while aurei and denarii of Q. Rustius (not a regular *tresvir a. a. a. f. f.*) *c.*19 BC show respectively the *clupeus virtutis* (see no. 4 above) juxtaposed, somewhat awkwardly, with the statue of Victory in the Senate House, and the altar of Fortuna Redux erected in Augustus' honour EX S C (*Fast. Amit.* under 12 October) and dedicated two months later (*Fast. Cum.* under 15 December) to celebrate his return from the east in 19 BC. By contrast, Augustus' *aes* coinage of Rome regularly bore the formula S C, which continued with rare exceptions (see no. 27 below) to appear on imperial *aes* down to the reign of Gallienus in the middle of the third century (*RIC* V (1), pp. 164 ff.). Non-imperial *aes* of Augustus and his successors did not bear the mark S C except for that of Syrian Antioch (*RIC* I², pp. 83 f.), the reason for which is not clear.

It has been suggested, though not convincingly, that S C on Augustus' *aes* of Rome refers to the honours—laurels, *corona civica*, *tribunicia potestas*, and the very title *Augustus* (see *a–c*)—shown on those coins (cf. K. Kraft in *Jahrb. für Num. und Geldgesch.* 1962, pp. 7 ff.). This theory (accepted by Griffin, *Nero*, p. 59) does not explain the S C associated with the types of Augustan quadrantes (see *d*) or the association in subsequent reigns of S C with a great mass of plainly non-honorific types. Nor, among other suggestions, is it possible to accept the theory of A. Bay (*JRS* 1972, pp. 111 ff.) that S C on Augustan *aes* called public attention to the bimetallic character of Augustus' new token coinage, brass for sestertii and dupondii, copper for asses and quadrantes. That might have served a purpose in Augustus' own time, but scarcely one or two hundred years later, when the bimetallic distinction was in any case often non-existent. Least probable of all is the old view (cf. Mattingly in *BMCRE* I, p. xvi) that S C indicated the senate's privilege of striking *aes*.

Tacitus' record of imperial intervention in the control of the *aerarium* (for which cf. Griffin, *Nero*, pp. 56f.: the basic intention may have been the search for responsible men able to resist debilitating demands from senior officials, cf. Tac. *Ann.* 1. 75) is impressive: under Augustus, *praefecti* in 28 BC (Dio Cass. 53. 2), praetors in 23 BC (Dio Cass. 53. 32); *praefecti* perhaps once more by AD 31 (unless the *praefectus* of Tac. *Ann.* 5. 8 was in fact a praetor 'put in charge' of the *aerarium*); the long-traditional quaestors in AD 44; ex-praetors under Nero in AD 56. It must be taken as certain that from Augustus onward the Princeps retained that control of gold and silver bullion and coin in the *aerarium* which had been effectively seized by Julius Caesar (above, no. 1), and it may be safely supposed that the senate retained the control of the militarily and economically less important *aes*. In the second century BC the keys of the *aerarium* were held by the quaestors (Polybius 23. 14). From Augustus onward they were held by men who were virtually imperial appointees; but now, when *aes* coinage at Rome was required and ordered (presumably after imperial suggestion amounting to command), we may nevertheless suppose that it was the senate which had to authorize the physical withdrawal of *aes* from the *aerarium*, and that it marked the *aes* thus coined with the formula S C. This view is strengthened by the apparent significance of the formula EX S C on the aurei and denarii of Nero from AD 54 to 64 (see no. **36** below). It may be argued, alternatively, that, while the senate *officially* retained control of coinage in all metals, *effective* control of it all lay with the Princeps, who courteously acknowledged the senate's right to withdraw *aes* for coinage and even, in the case of the young Nero, went to the extreme of such courtesy for gold and silver as well. If the general extent of imperial power and monopoly is, however, taken into account, this view is perhaps less likely to be true.

By contrast, the S C on the African denarii of Clodius Macer's short revolt (see no. **42**) and on those of Galba, probably also produced in Africa (*RIC* I², pp. 193ff., 215), alluded to the claim that Macer and Galba were coining in the political interest of the senate.

15. Tiberius and Divus Augustus

1. Tac. *Ann.* 1. 11. Versae inde ad Tiberium preces. Et ille varie disserebat de magnitudine imperii, sua modestia. Solam divi Augusti mentem tantae molis capacem: se in partem curarum ab illo vocatum experiendo didicisse quam arduum, quam subiectum fortunae regendi cuncta onus. Proinde in civitate tot inlustribus viris subnixa non ad unum omnia deferrent: plures facilius munia rei publicae sociatis laboribus exsecuturos. Plus in oratione tali dignitatis quam fidei erat (of AD 14).

2. Suet. *Tib.* 24. Principatum, quamvis neque occupare confestim neque agere dubitasset, ... diu tamen recusavit, impudentissimo mimo nunc adhortantis amicos increpans ut ignaros, quanta belua esset imperium, nunc precantem senatum ... ambiguis responsis et callida cunctatione suspendens.

3. Vell. Pat. 2. 124. 2. Una tamen veluti luctatio civitatis fuit, pugnantis cum Caesare senatus populique romani ut stationi paternae succederet, illius ut potius aequalem civem quam eminentem liceret agere principem. Tandem magis ratione quam honore victus est, cum quicquid tuendum non suscepisset periturum videret.

Tac. *Ann.* 1. 11. After this the prayers turned to Tiberius. He held forth, with various arguments, about the great size of the empire and about his own limitations. Only the intellect of the divine Augustus, he said, was equal to so huge a task: he himself had been called to share the cares of empire by Augustus, and experience had taught him how difficult the burden of universal rule was, and how much at the mercy of fortune. Therefore, he said, in a state supported by so many distinguished men they should not lay everything on one man: if more of them shared in the labours they would the more easily carry out the public business. His speech certainly had dignity, but it scarcely rang true.

Suet. *Tib.* 24. For some long time, however, he refused the principate, though he had entertained no doubt either about accepting it at once or of performing the duty. He really acted a shameless part, now upbraiding his backers for their ignorance of the brute size of the empire, now leaving the importunate senate in suspense as a result of his ambiguous answers and his cunning hesitation.

Vell. Pat. 2. 124. 2. You could say, however, that one civil struggle took place. The senate and people fought with Caesar to persuade him to succeed to his father's position, while Caesar fought for the freedom to conduct his principate as an ordinary citizen and not from a position of eminence. Finally, reason prevailed over honour, when he saw that what he did not protect would perish.

15a   **15f**

a *RIC* I², p. 99, no. 72. As of Rome, *c*.AD 15–16. *Obv.* DIVVS AVGVSTVS PATER, Head of Augustus with radiate crown, star, and thunderbolt. *Rev.* S C, Draped female figure holding patera and sceptre.

b *RIC* I², p. 99, no. 77. Dupondius of Rome, *c*.AD 22–3. *Obv.* DIVVS AVGVSTVS PATER, Head of Augustus with radiate crown. *Rev.* S C, Victory with shield inscribed S P Q R.

c *RIC* I², p. 99, no. 79. Dupondius of Rome, *c*.AD 22–3 onwards. *Obv.* DIVVS AVGVSTVS PATER, Head of Augustus with radiate crown. *Rev.* S C in oak-wreath.

d *RIC* I², p. 99, no. 81. As of Rome, *c*.AD 22–3 onwards. *Obv.* DIVVS AVGVSTVS PATER, Head of Augustus with radiate crown. *Rev.* S C, PROVIDENT(*ia*), Altar.

e *RIC* I², p. 99, no. 83. As of Rome, *c*.AD 34–7. *Obv.* DIVVS AVGVSTVS PATER, Head of Augustus with radiate crown. *Rev.* S C, Winged thunderbolt.

f *RIC* I², p. 98, no. 69. Sestertius of Rome, AD 36–7. *Obv.* DIVO AVGVSTO S P Q R, Shield inscribed OB CIVES SER(*vatos*) in oak-wreath supported by capricorns above globe. *Rev.* TI(*berius*) CAESAR DIVI AVG(*usti*) F(*ilius*) AVGVST(*us*) P(*ontifex*) M(*aximus*) TR(*ibunicia*) POT(*estate*) XXXIIX around S C.

Tiberius had been adopted by Augustus as his son, and thus also as his heir, in AD 4 (*Fast. Amit.* under 26 June; cf. Vell. Pat. 2. 103) after the death of Gaius Caesar, his last surviving adopted grandson (see no. 10 above). Although rumour held that subsequent relations between Augustus and Tiberius were scarcely cordial (cf. Suet. *Tib.* 21. 2), and although no coinage emphasized Tiberius' now eminent position until AD 10–11 at Rome (*RIC* I², p. 78) and AD 13–14 at Lugdunum (ibid., p. 56), from AD 4 Tiberius faced the certain prospect of succession if he survived Augustus, who was older by 21 years. Devoid of any drop of Julian blood, this son of Augustus' widely revered wife Livia was to spend the next decade in the shadow of Augustus—the military man in the shadow of the skilled political administrator. His apparent hesitation when the principate was delivered to him in AD 14 was interpreted by later historians with suspicion about his sincerity. But it may well have arisen from a now absolute appreciation of the *mens*, the intellect, of the dead Augustus, who had had such long and profound experience of imperial administration (cf. Vell. Pat. 2. 131. 1, and see P. A. Brunt in *CQ* 1984, pp. 423–44, esp. pp. 424 f.)— an experience which he had not perhaps shared sufficiently from AD 4 with Tiberius. However devious and ill-seeming Tiberius' attitude to the senate may have appeared in AD 14 (and on this see the differing views of Seager, *Tiberius*, pp. 48–52, and Levick, *TP*, ch. V; also P. A. Brunt in *JRS* 1977, pp. 97 f.), it would be unwise to doubt his admiration of Augustus as Princeps. Strong evidence for this is to be seen in the *aes* coinage of Rome from AD 14 to 37. A very large proportion of this coinage consisted of commemorative dupondii and asses (the everyday currency of the ordinary man) in honour of Divus Augustus: these made reference to his deification, his *corona civica* and his *clupeus virtutis* (see no. 4 above), and (on sestertii at the end of Tiberius' reign) even his capricorn birth-sign. These commemorative coins were produced in not less than five separate stages (cf. *RIC* I², pp. 88 ff.; a different and less probable chronology is proposed by W. Szaivert in *Die*

Münzprägung der Kaiser Tiberius und Caius, Vienna, 1984, pp. 37 f.); and in the aggregate they must certainly have formed a very substantial proportion of Tiberius' current *aes* coinage. It could of course be argued that the *aes* coinage of Rome was not yet sufficiently under imperial control to reflect imperial thinking; but, even if that might have been true of Augustan *aes* down to *c.*4 BC (cf. *RIC* I², pp. 65–78), total change had taken place by AD 10–12 in all the outward forms (id., p. 78, nos. 469–71) and thus presumably in the policy which dictated the change. There is no obvious sign of senatorial (as distinct from imperial) choice of coin-types for *aes* under Tiberius, and there was to be none under Gaius. The 'Divus Augustus' types on Tiberius' *aes* may therefore be a direct reflection of Tiberius' keen (and uncomfortable) awareness of Augustus' political sagacity. Tiberius' initial hesitation, unintelligible or suspect in the eyes of a Tacitus or a Suetonius, is not so surprising in the longer perspective of history.

16. Army unrest under Tiberius in AD 14

1. Tac. *Ann.* 1. 16 f. Pannonicas legiones seditio incessit . . . Lascivire miles, discordare, pessimi cuiusque sermonibus praebere auris . . . Satis per tot annos ignavia peccatum, quod tricena aut quadragena stipendia senes . . . tolerent. Ne dimissis quidem finem esse militiae, sed apud vexillum tendentis alio vocabulo eosdem labores perferre . . . Enimvero militiam ipsam gravem, infructuosam: denis in diem assibus animam et corpus aestimari: hinc vestem arma tentoria, hinc saevitiam centurionum . . . redimi . . . Nec aliud levamentum quam si certis sub legibus militia iniretur, ut singulos denarios mererent, sextus decumus stipendii annus finem adferret (of AD 14).

Tac. *Ann.* 1. 16 f. Sedition spread among the legions of Pannonia. The troops lost discipline, quarrelled, and gave ear to whatever the riff-raff said. 'We have been cowardly fools for so many years, putting up, as old men, with thirty or forty years' service. There's no end to military service even on our discharge, for we carry on the same work, under another name, serving with the standards . . . Military service is indeed hard, and unrewarding: our body and soul are valued at ten asses a day, and from this we have to buy clothing, arms, and tents,

and buy off the cruelty of the centurions too . . . The only relief can
come from fixed rules of military service—a denarius a day, and a
limit of sixteen years in the army.'

16a

16c

a C. M. Kraay in *Essays . . . Mattingly*, pl. VI, no. 1. As of Augustus.
Obv. Head of Augustus, greatly worn; countermark TIB · IM
(*Tiberius imperator*).

b Ibid., pl. VI, no. 2. As of Augustus. *Obv.* Head of Augustus, greatly
worn; countermarks, in sequence, CÆ (*Caesar*) over TIB(*erius*).

c Ibid., pl. VI, no. 3. As of Augustus. *Obv.* Head of Augustus, greatly
worn; countermarks, in sequence, IMP · AVG (*Imperator Augustus*)
over TIB · AVG (*Tiberius Augustus*).

Tiberius' accession was followed quickly by serious unrest,
verging on mutiny, among the three legions in Pannonia, and
the efforts of his son Drusus were necessary to restore order (cf.
Seager, *Tiberius*, pp. 58–71, and Campbell, *ERA*, pp. 370f.). A
principal complaint of the disaffected soldiers was the length of
military service, raised *c.*AD 6, for reasons of economy, from
sixteen years with four in the reserve to twenty years with five in
the reserve (Dio Cass. 55. 23. 1). Added to this there was the
brutality of the centurions, and the rate of pay. Common
soldiers now received 10 asses per day, = 3600 asses =
225 denarii per year of 360 days, and they were demanding
16 asses (= 1 denarius) per day, i.e. 360 denarii per year—an
increase of over 50 per cent. Parallel unrest broke out almost
simultaneously among the legions of the Rhine, and the
complaints were the same: *venisse tempus quo veterani maturam
missionem, iuvenes largiora stipendia, cuncti modum miseriarum
exposcerent saevitiamque centurionum ulciscerentur* (Tac. *Ann.* 1. 31).
There is no evidence of any change in the rate of military pay
until Domitian increased it from 225 to 300 denarii per year
(Suet. *Dom.* 7. 3), and the personal authority of Drusus in

Pannonia and of Germanicus on the Rhine allayed the present trouble, which may have been caused partly by the change of *princeps* (cf. the *mutatus princeps* of Tac. *Ann.* 1. 16, and the willingness of the Rhine legions to see Germanicus displace Tiberius as Augustus' successor, Tac. *Ann.* 1. 35).

A conspicuous feature of the abundant *aes* found at the military establishments strung northwards along the Rhine from Vindonissa to Mogontiacum (Mainz) is the quantity of asses, still mainly of the 'moneyers'' series of Augustus and thus much worn, with one or another variant of a Tiberian countermark (see C. M. Kraay in *Essays . . . Mattingly*, pp. 113 ff.). These countermarks may to some degree reflect the need felt at Rome to validate a greatly worn and indeed sometimes almost illegible coinage current along the military bases of the Rhine until fresh supplies could be struck. But they may equally reflect Tiberius' desire, loyally backed by Germanicus (cf. Tac. *Ann.* 1. 35, *ille moriturum potius quam fidem exueret clamitans*), to emphasize his own position and authority as the new *imperator*, the new commander-in-chief of the armies, the new *Augustus*, the new *princeps*. The countermarks certainly provided a phenomenon of an intensity never seen before or afterwards. Whatever the reason for them, the unrest among the legions both on the Rhine and in Pannonia subsided, though not without having caused considerable unease in Rome itself (Tac. *Ann.* 1. 46).

17. *Tribunicia potestas* on the coinage of Tiberius

1. Tac. *Ann.* 3. 57. Praeceperant animis orationem patres quo quaesitior adulatio fuit. Nec tamen repertum nisi ut effigies principum, aras deum, templa et arcus aliaque solita censerent, nisi quod M. Silanus ex contumelia consulatus honorem principibus petivit dixitque pro sententia ut publicis privatisve monimentis ad memoriam temporum non consulum nomina praescriberentur, sed eorum qui tribuniciam potestatem gererent (of AD 22).

Tac. *Ann.* 3. 57. The senators had anticipated this speech, and so their flattery could be the more elaborate. But they could find nothing to vote about save imperial portraits, altars of the gods, temples, arches, and all the usual things, except that M. Silanus sought to honour the princes by means of a slur on the consulship. He proposed that public and private monuments should be inscribed not with the names of consuls, to mark their date, but with the names of those who held tribunician power.

a *RIC* I², p. 95, no. 25. Aureus of Lugdunum, AD 14–37. *Obv.* TI(*berius*) CAESAR DIVI AVG(*usti*) F(*ilius*) AVGVSTVS, Head of Tiberius, laureate. *Rev.* PONTIF(*ex*) MAXIM(*us*), Seated female figure holding sceptre and branch.

b *RIC* I², p. 93, no. 5. Gold quinarius of Lugdunum, AD 15–16. *Obv.* TI(*berius*) DIVI F(*ilius*) AVGVSTVS, Head of Tiberius, laureate. *Rev.* TR(*ibunicia*) POT(*estate*) XVII, Victory with wreath seated on globe.

c *RIC* I², p. 97, no. 44. As of Rome, AD 22–3. *Obv.* TI(*berius*) CAESAR DIVI AVG(*usti*) F(*ilius*) AVGVST(*us*) IMP(*erator*) VIII, Head of Tiberius, bare. *Rev.* PONTIF(*ex*) MAXIM(*us*) TRIBVN(*icia*) POTEST(*ate*) XXIIII around S C.

d *RIC* I², p. 97, no. 45. As of Rome, AD 22–3. *Obv.* DRVSVS CAESAR TI(*berii*) AVG(*usti*) F(*ilius*) DIVI AVG(*usti*) N(*epos*), Head of Drusus, bare. *Rev.* PONTIF(*ex*) TRIBVN(*icia*) POTEST(*ate*) ITER(*um*) around S C.

In AD 22 Tiberius formally requested *tribunicia potestas* (on which see W. K. Lacey in *JRS* 1979, pp. 28–34) from the senate for his son Drusus, emphasizing his success as a military commander and the fact that he had twice been consul and was also a family man (Tac. *Ann.* 3. 56; cf. Rogers, *SRT*, pp. 130–2). Tacitus outlined, not without mockery, the senate's predictable reaction. He does not give us Tiberius' response to Silanus' novel suggestion (which ran contrary to all previous convention), but the subsequent coinage suggests that it was at least partially adopted. The *aes* coinage of Tiberius from the mint of Rome had begun, in AD 15–16, with tribunician dating (see *RIC* I², p. 96, nos. 33–7) but dropped it between then and AD 20–1 (*RIC* I², p. 97, nos. 38–40). Tribunician dating, momentarily evident on extremely rare *aes* of AD 20–1 (*RIC* I², p. 97, no. 41), was fully restored in AD 22–3, not only for Tiberius (see *c*) but also on *aes* in honour of Drusus (see *d*), and was thereafter constant on Tiberius' *aes* of Rome from AD 34 to 37 (*RIC* I², pp. 97 f., nos. 52–69). It did not of course appear on the very common *aes* of Rome with 'Divus Augustus' types (*RIC* I², pp. 98 f., nos. 70–83), where it would have been anachronistic and incorrect: not until the Flavian period was this difficulty neatly solved by adding to such commemorative types the dated legend of the current *princeps* with the addition of REST(*ituit*) or RESTITVIT (*RIC* II, pp. 141 ff.). What seems therefore to have been an ultimately systematic adoption of tribunician dating on Tiberius' *aes* from the mint of Rome was not, however, paralleled on the vast series of aurei and denarii struck for him at Lugdunum (see no. 9 above). There a tribunician dating appeared only on a few rare coins of AD 14–16, and on the series of even rarer gold quinarii from AD 15–16 down to AD 36–7 (*RIC* I², pp. 93 f., nos. 1–22): the immense PONTIF MAXIM series of gold and silver, lasting probably from AD 14 to 37, and now constituting perhaps the most frequent of all Julio-Claudian precious-metal coinages, lacks any date, its relative chronology depending only on the observation of the steadily ageing features of Tiberius and of certain inconstant details of the reverse type of the seated (?)Pax or (?)Livia (*RIC* I², p. 95, nos. 25–30; cf. *BMCRE* I, pp. cxxx f. and B. Lichocka, *Justitia sur les monnaies impériales* (Warsaw, 1974), pp. 87 f.). A decision on tribunician dating taken by the senate at Rome, and reflected on the *aes* of the mint of Rome, would not affect the imperially controlled mint of Lugdunum. It would have been the citizens of Rome and of Italy who would have been chiefly aware of the conceptual significance of *tribunicia potestas*—a power designed for the protection of the people (Tac. *Ann.* 1. 2). And an alert bureaucracy would have been quick to realize that the annual dating of at least some coinage by the imperial tenure of *tribunicia potestas* enabled a closer check to be kept on the standards of quality and weight (for a more comprehensive view of which subject see Sutherland, *Rev. Belge* 1984, pp. 49 ff.).

18. Tiberius and the earthquake in Roman Asia

1. Tac. *Ann.* 2. 47. Eodem anno duodecim celebres Asiae urbes conlapsae nocturno motu terrae, quo improvisior graviorque pestis fuit ... Sedisse inmensos montis, visa in arduo quae plana fuerint, effulsisse inter ruinam ignis memorant. Asperrima in Sardianos lues plurimum in eosdem misericordiae traxit: nam centies sestertium pollicitus Caesar, et quantum aerario aut fisco pendebant in quinquennium remisit (of AD 17).

2. Suet. *Tib.* 48. 2. Ne provincias quidem liberalitate ulla sublevavit, excepta Asia, disiectis terrae motu civitatibus.

Tac. *Ann.* 2. 47. In that same year twelve famous cities of Asia were wrecked by an earthquake in the night, so that disaster was all the more sudden and serious. Stories recount how great hills subsided, and that what had been level seemed to rear up, and that fires blazed among the ruin. The most acute damage fell on the people of Sardis, and they attracted most sympathy, shown by the emperor's promise to them of ten million sesterces and by his five-year remission of all their dues to the public or the imperial exchequer.

Suet. *Tib.* 48. 2. He did not help even the provinces with any act of generosity, except for Asia, when cities had been torn apart by an earthquake.

18a

a RIC I², p. 97, no. 48. Sestertius of Rome, AD 22–3. *Obv.* CIVITA-
TIBVS ASIAE RESTITVTIS, Tiberius seated, laureate, holding
patera and sceptre. *Rev.* TI(*berius*) CAESAR DIVI AVG(*usti*)
F(*ilius*) AVGVST(*us*) P(*ontifex*) M(*aximus*) TR(*ibunicia*)
POT(*estate*) XXIIII around S C.

Tacitus, who was not deeply interested in the social or
economic welfare of the provinces, clearly recorded the damage
to twelve cities of the province of Asia by the earthquake of
AD 17, with Sardis as the principal sufferer, closely followed by
Magnesia. A second, if less severe, earthquake seems to have
occurred in AD 20 (cf. Grant, *RAI*, p. 66). Tiberius promised
10 million sesterces (= $2\frac{1}{2}$ million denarii = 100,000 aurei) by
way of relief to Sardis alone, while also remitting its dues to the
aerarium and the *fiscus* for five years. His relief-grants as a whole
(see Seager, *Tiberius*, pp. 172 f., and P. A. Brunt in *JRS* 1981,
p. 169) were commemorated by acts of civic thanks (Grant,
ibid. and the Puteoli monument of AD 30, *E. and J.*², ch. III,
no. 50 = *ILS* 156). The scale of financial help, either immediate or through five-year remissions of tax-dues, to all twelve
cities is not specified by Tacitus, but it must have been very
great.

Significantly, it was not until five years had passed that the
reasonably large issue of fine sestertii from the mint of Rome
commemorated the restoration of the shattered cities. Those
five years had doubtless been taken up in rebuilding. This fact
was not appreciated by Woodman in his commentary on Vell.
Pat. 2. 126. 4 (p. 243), while Grant (*RAI*, p. 66) erroneously
assigned these sestertii to *c.*AD 30, proceeding on the theory
(afterwards disproved by Sutherland, *CRIP*, pp. 191 ff.) that a
coin dated TR POT XXIIII could have been *authorized*, but

not actually issued, in AD 22–3. The end of the tax-free quinquennium, coinciding with the essential completion of the
physical reconstruction of the damaged cities, was the apt
moment for the issue at Rome of the *aes* sestertii—the sestertius
was an emphatically metropolitan denomination—on which
Tiberius, the provincial benefactor, was shown in civilian dress,
holding the patera of religious observance.

19. Tiberius' annexation of Cappadocia, and the Sales Tax under Tiberius and Gaius

1. *RG* 17. 2. Et M. Lepido et L. Arruntio consulibus (= AD 6) in
aerarium militare quod ex consilio meo constitutum est, ex quo
praemia darentur militibus qui vicena aut plura stipendia emeruissent, HS (= sestertium) milliens et septingentiens ex patrimonio meo
detuli.

2. Tac. *Ann.* 2. 42. Rex Archelaus quinquagesimum annum
Cappadocia potiebatur, invisus Tiberio quod eium Rhodi agentem
nullo officio coluisset ... Regnum in provinciam redactum est,
fructibusque eius levari posse centesimae vectigal professus Caesar
ducentesimam in posterum statuit (of AD 17).

3. Dio Cass. 58. 16. 1f. καὶ γὰρ τὰ χρήματα δι᾽ ἀκριβείας ἤδη πολὺ
μᾶλλον ἐποιεῖτο. καὶ διὰ τοῦτο καὶ τέλος τι διακοσιοστὴν ἔχον ἑκατοστὴν
ἤγαγε (of AD 31).

4. Suet. *Gaius* 16. 3. Ducentesimam auctionum Italiae remisit.

RG 17. 2. And in the consulship of M. Lepidus and L. Arruntius I
paid 170 million sesterces from my family fortune into the military
treasury which I had decided to set up for the payment of gratuities to
ex-soldiers with twenty or more years of service.

Tac. *Ann.* 2. 42. King Archelaus had been in possession of Cappadocia for twenty years. He was disliked by Tiberius because he had
shown him no mark of respect during Tiberius' time at Rhodes ...
Tiberius reduced his kingdom to the status of a province, and, declar-
ing that the 1% tax could be lightened as a result of its revenues, set it
for the future at ½%.

Dio Cass. 58. 16. 1 f. For by accurate management he (Tiberius) was greatly increasing capital, and consequently set a certain tax, previously of ½%, at 1%.

Suet. *Gaius* 16. 3. He (Gaius) remitted the ½% sales tax for Italy.

a *RIC* I², p. 100, no. 86. Silver drachma of Caesarea in Cappadocia, AD 33–4. *Obv.* TI(*berius*) CAESAR AVG(*ustus*) P(*ontifex*) M(*aximus*) ℞(*ibunicia*) P(*otestate*) XXXV, Head of Tiberius, laureate. *Rev.* DRVSVS CAES(*ar*) TI(*berii*) AVG(*usti*) F(*ilius*) COS II ℞(*ibunicia*) P(*otestate*) IT(*erum*), Head of Drusus, bare.

b *RIC* I², p. 111, no. 45. Quadrans of Rome, AD 39–40. *Obv.* C CAESAR DIVI AVG(*usti*) PRON(*epos*) AVG(*ustus*), Cap of freedom between S C. *Rev.* PON(*tifex*) M(*aximus*) TR(*ibunicia*) P(*otestate*) III P(*ater*) P(*atriae*) COS TERT around R(*emissa*) CC (= *ducentesima*).

In AD 6 Augustus had instituted the *aerarium militare* for the payment of military pensions (cf. Suet. *Div. Aug.* 49. 2), feeding it thereafter with the *vicesima hereditatium* (5% inheritance tax) and the *centesima rerum venalium* (1% sales tax) (cf. Tac. *Ann.* 1. 78 and Dio Cass. 55. 25. 5). Tiberius' act in AD 17 of dispossessing Archelaus of the kingdom of Cappadocia (for the wealth of which cf. M. Pani, *Roma e i re d'Oriente da Augusto a Tiberio* (Bari, n.d.), pp. 142 f.) enabled him to halve the sales tax to ½% (*ducentesima*). According to Dio Cassius, it was Tiberius' careful sense of finance that led him in AD 31 to raise it to the original figure of 1%. However, between 31 and 39 it had evidently been halved once again (unless Suetonius' *auctionum* is to be given some special and limited meaning), for the tax-remission recorded both by Suetonius and also by Gaius' coinage from 39 (see *b*) is that of a *ducentesima*, ½%. If the figures given by Tacitus, Suetonius, and Dio Cassius are correct—and they are not mutually inconsistent—it has to be supposed that varying costs incurred by the *aerarium militare* had to be balanced by variation of income.

It may well be the case that the annexation of Cappadocia, and the inflow of what were now its provincial revenues to Rome, constituted one reason for the establishment of the new imperial mint of Caesarea (see no. 21), which was to coin drachmae or didrachms for the rest of the Julio-Claudian period with Latin legends, changed thereafter to Greek.

20. Livia's serious illness in AD 22

1. Tac. *Ann.* 3. 64. Sub idem tempus Iuliae Augustae valetudo atrox necessitudinem principi fecit festinati in urbem reditus, sincera adhuc inter matrem filiumque concordia sive occultis odiis. Neque enim multo ante, cum haud procul theatro Marcelli effigiem divo Augusto Iulia dicaret, Tiberi nomen suo postscripserat, idque ille credebatur ut inferius maiestate principis gravi et dissimulata offensione abdidisse (of AD 22).

Tac. *Ann.* 3. 64. At about the same time Julia Augusta was dreadfully ill, and the emperor was compelled to hurry back to Rome: until now relations between mother and son had been genuinely harmonious, unless it was that hatred was concealed. For not long before, Julia, in dedicating an effigy of Augustus not far from the theatre of Marcellus, had inscribed Tiberius' name below her own, and rumour had it that Tiberius had hidden his deep sense of offence at what he regarded as a slight to his great position.

20a

a RIC I², p. 97, no. 51. Sestertius of Rome, AD 22–3. *Obv.* S P Q R IVLIAE AVGVST(*ae*), Carpentum ornamented with Victories and other figures and drawn by two mules. *Rev.* TI(*berius*)

CAESAR DIVI AVG(*usti*) F(*ilius*) AVGVST(*us*) P(*ontifex*) M(*aximus*) TR(*ibunicia*) POT(*estate*) XXIIII around S C.

Livia's illness in AD 22, at the advanced age of 79, was serious enough to bring Tiberius back in haste from Campania, whither he had withdrawn the year before (Tac. *Ann.* 3. 31): in a deliberately half-hearted fashion Tacitus admits the possibility of genuine good feeling between the *princeps* and his mother. As the widow of Augustus and (Suet. *Div. Aug.* 101. 2) co-heir with Tiberius to his fortune, she was the deeply venerated link with that recent and golden past (cf. Vell. Pat. 2. 130. 5), and could be styled Genetrix Orbis in Spain, Πρόνοια in Athens, and Ἑστία νέα in Lampsacus (*E. and J.*², nos. 123 f., 128 f.; for the cults in her honour cf. S. R. F. Price, *Rituals and Power* (Cambridge, 1984), s.v. Livia). The Sardonyx Cameo (*CAH* X, p. 634 with *CAH* Plates IV, p. 156) shows Tiberius only slightly higher than Livia. To what extent Tiberius grudged her such eminence is not easy to determine from a literary tradition which often fed keenly on scandalous rumour, but Tacitus clearly suggests an easily offended dignity, and Suetonius (*Tib.* 50. 2) wrote of his irritation with Livia *velut partes sibi aequas potentiae vindicantem*. On the occasion of her acute illness, however, full public recognition of her great status was accorded. When she recovered, the senate decreed *supplicationes* to the gods, with *ludi magni* in Rome (Tac. *Ann.* 3.64), and could certainly not have taken such action without Tiberius' approval (cf. Tac. *Ann.* 1. 14). Moreover, the mint of Rome, now no longer a free agent (see no. 14 above), struck two issues of fine sestertii in AD 22–3 (Tiberius as *tr. p. XXIIII*) which would have enjoyed a currency principally in Rome and Italy. These clearly celebrated Livia's recovery—she was not to die until AD 29 (Tac. *Ann.* 5. 1)—and show what is part of a processional scene, perhaps a part of the *supplicationes* decreed by the senate, in which a *carpentum* (a two-wheeled and curtained wagon for ceremonial use by ladies of note; cf. Livy 5. 25) is featured. The curtains do not allow us to tell whether on this occasion the aged convalescent rode in it.

Mattingly has pointed out (*BMCRE* I, p. cxxxv) that, although there is evidence of the grant to Messallina to ride in a *carpentum* (Suet. *Div. Claud.* 17. 3), as also to the younger

Agrippina (Tac. *Ann.* 12. 42), no such privilege is recorded for
Livia except by these sestertii. In his reference to Agrippina
Tacitus defines the processional *carpentum* as an *honos sacer-
dotibus et sacris* (i.e. images of the gods) *antiquitus concessus*, but
C. L. Clay has commented (*Num. Zeitschr.* 1982, pp. 28 f., with
note 80) on the difference between a *carpentum* and a *tensa*, the
latter of which bore divine figures.

21. The death of Tiberius' son Drusus

1. Tac. *Ann.* 4. 3. Ceterum plena Caesarum domus, iuvenis filius,
nepotes adulti moram cupitis adferebant; et quia vi tot simul
corripere intutum dolus intervalla scelerum poscebat. Placuit tamen
occultior via et a Druso incipere, in quem recenti ira ferebatur
(Seianus).

2. Tac. *Ann.* 4. 8. Igitur Seianus maturandum ratus deligit venenum
quo paulatim inrepente fortuitus morbus adsimularetur. Id Druso
datum per Lygdum spadonem, ut octo post annos cognitum est (of
AD 23).

Tac. *Ann.* 4. 3. But the imperial house had checks to Sejanus'
ambitions in the form of many princes, a son in young manhood, and
grown-up grandsons. It was unsafe to sweep away so many by
sudden violence. Cunning therefore demanded a series of crimes. So
he preferred the way of stealth, and began with Drusus, against
whom his anger had been lately aroused.

Tac. *Ann.* 4. 8. Sejanus thought that there was no time to be lost. He
chose a poison of which the gradual working might give the appearance of a natural disease. It came to light eight years later that it was
administered by the eunuch Lygdus.

21a

a RIC I², p. 100, no. 85. Silver drachma of Caesarea in Cappadocia,
AD 32–3. *Obv.* TI(*berius*) CAES(*ar*) AVG(*ustus*) P(*ontifex*) M(*aximus*) R(*ibunicia*) P(*otestate*) XXXIV, Head of Tiberius, laureate.

Rev. DRVSVS CAES(*ar*) TI(*berii*) AVG(*usti*) F(*ilius*) COS II ᵀR(*ibunicia*) P(*otestate*), Head of Drusus, bare.

Drusus, son of Tiberius, had held tribunician power for the second time (see *RIC* I², p. 97, no. 45; and above, no. **19a**) in AD 23–4 (*PIR²* I, p. 219). His military experience and campaigning success were considerable (Tac. *Ann.* 1. 24 ff.; 2. 43 f.; 3. 7); his wife Livia (Livilla) had borne him twin sons in AD 19 (Tac. *Ann.* 2. 84), thus ensuring dynastic succession; and his own position as successor to Tiberius seemed equally sure (Tac. *Ann.* 3. 56; cf. Rogers, *SRT*, pp. 102–36). Opposed to him was the formidable ambition of L. Aelius Sejanus, appointed co-prefect of the Praetorian Guard with his father Seius Strabo in AD 14, and not long thereafter sole prefect of the Guard (see D. Hennig in *Vestigia* 21, Munich, 1975, pp. 19 f.), whose cohorts, previously scattered throughout Rome, he concentrated for their (and his own) increased authority and influence within a single barracks (Tac. *Ann.* 4. 2). Sejanus, though no more than an *eques*, now aimed at being the *adiutor* of Tiberius (Tac. *Ann.* 4. 7) in the *principalia onera* (Vell. Pat. 2. 127. 3; cf. Dio Cass. 57. 19), and to that end he undertook the destruction of Drusus and his family. First, he seduced Drusus' wife Livia, *quae soror Germanici . . . pulchritudine praecellebat* (Tac. *Ann.* 4. 3), and then he moved against Drusus himself. Velleius (2. 130. 3) passed over Drusus' death in a brief and rhetorically comprehensive phrase, and indeed doubts have been expressed about his murder (cf. Rogers, *SRT*, pp. 137–40; Hennig, *Seianus*, pp. 33–40; and Seager, *Tiberius*, pp. 181–87). Tacitus (*Ann.* 4. 10 f.), like Dio Cassius (57. 22. 1–4), rejected any view that Tiberius was privy to his son's murder, or that he contributed by negligence to his death. Indeed, Tacitus represents Tiberius as being almost unnaturally strong in the face of Drusus' lingering death.

The lost body of Book 5 of the *Annals* would have indicated in some detail Tiberius' reaction to the knowledge, gained by the torture of Lygdus, that Sejanus had engineered Drusus' death: Suetonius (*Tib.* 62) notes his savage anger. Public recognition of Drusus' good name was, however, to be made in the year following Lygdus' confession. This occurred at the mint of Caesarea in Cappadocia, which Tiberius had annexed in AD 17 (see no. **19** above). This mint, which produced silver drachmae or didrachms, presumably for eastern military pay, throughout most of the Julio-Claudian period (cf. *RIC* I², pp. 112 f., 131 f., 185 f.), in AD 32–3 struck drachmae with a reverse showing Drusus' portrait with a legend appropriate for AD 23, the year of his death, and a similar issue followed in AD 33–4 (*RIC* I², p. 100, nos. 86 f.). The Julio-Claudian coinage provides no other such instance of fortuitously decennial commemoration. Mattingly has suggested (*BMCRE* I, p. cxli) that this coinage was produced in connection with L. Vitellius' eastern operations (Tac. *Ann.* 6. 31 f.; cf. Dio Cass. 58. 26); but these came a little later than the coinage, which might however have been an aspect of forward military planning. In any event, an essentially military mint now commemorates an essentially military man ten years after his brutal murder by Sejanus.

22. The *potentia* of Sejanus

1. Tac. *Ann.* 4. 1 f. Mox Tiberium variis artibus devixit (Sejanus) adeo ut obscurum adversum alios sibi uni incautum intectumque efficeret . . . Vim praefecturae (sc. praetorio) modicam antea intendit, dispersas per urbem cohortis una in castra conducendo . . . Ut perfecta sunt castra, inrepere paulatim militaris animos adeundo, appellando . . . Neque senatorio ambitu abstinebat clientes suos honoribus aut provinciis ornandi, facili Tiberio atque ita prono ut socium laborum non modo in sermonibus, sed apud patres et populum celebraret coliqueper theatra et fora effigies eius interque principia legionum sineret (of AD 23).

Tac. *Ann.* 4. 1 f. Sejanus, with his mingled skills, soon won Tiberius over to the point at which, impenetrable to others, he showed himself open and unreserved to Sejanus alone . . . He concentrated the formerly moderate strength of the Praetorian Guard, scattered as the cohorts had been through Rome, by putting them into a single barracks . . . With the completion of the barracks he gradually exerted his influence over the soldiers' minds, mixing with the men and calling them by name . . . Nor was he slow in cultivating the senate: he rewarded his supporters with honours and provincial posts, and Tiberius was so easily influenced, so supine, that he praised Sejanus, not only in private conversation but even in speeches to the senate or the people, as his partner in work, and allowed his portraits to be honoured in theatres, forums, and legionary head-quarters.

22a

22c

a RIC I², p. 97, no. 42. Sestertius of Rome, AD 23. *Obv.* No legend. Confronting heads of Drusus' twin sons on crossed cornucopiae with caduceus between. *Rev.* DRVSVS CAESAR TI(*berii*) AVG(*usti*) F(*ilius*) DIVI AVG(*usti*) N(*epos*) PONT(*ifex*) TR(*ibunicia*) POT(*estate*) II around S C.

b RIC I², p. 97, no. 43. Dupondius of Rome, AD 23. *Obv.* PIETAS, Veiled and diademed bust of Pietas. *Rev.* DRVSVS CAESAR TI(*berii*) AVGVSTI F(*ilius*) TR(*ibunicia*) POT(*estate*) ITER(*um*) around S C.

c RIC I², p. 97, no. 46. Dupondius of Rome, AD 22–3. *Obv.* IVSTI-TIA, Diademed bust of Justitia. *Rev.* TI(*berius*) CAESAR DIVI AVG(*usti*) F(*ilius*) AVG(*ustus*) P(*ontifex*) M(*aximus*) TR(*ibunicia*) POT(*estate*) XXIIII around S C.

d RIC I², p. 97, no. 47. Dupondius of Rome, AD 22–3. *Obv.* SALVS AVGVSTA, Bust of Salus. *Rev.* TI(*berius*) CAESAR DIVI AVG(*usti*) F(*ilius*) AVG(*ustus*) TR(*ibunicia*) POT(*estate*) XXIIII around S C.

In AD 21 Tiberius withdrew from Rome to Campania (Tac. *Ann.* 3. 31), and the advancement in power of L. Aelius Sejanus, now for some time the sole *praefectus praetorio* (see no. **21** above) and thus already a prominent figure, gained speed. In the following year, 22, Sejanus received high praise from Tiberius (and a public statue from the senate) for his part in limiting the fire damage to the theatre of Pompey (Tac. *Ann.* 3. 72), and by 23 he consolidated his own power-base by concentrating the praetorian cohorts within a single barracks (Tac. *Ann.* 4. 2; dated to 20 by Dio Cass. 57. 19. 6, on which see R. Syme, *Tacitus*, Oxford, 1958, p. 286, note 2). According to Tacitus, from whom alone is derived a detailed account of Sejanus' character and rise (on which see D. Hennig, *Sejanus*, pp. 68–156, reviewed by B. Levick in *Class. Rev.* 1977, pp. 225 f.), it was from that same time that Sejanus' influence over Tiberius and the senate sharply increased, encouraging him to undertake in 23 a ruthless plan to destroy each of the two existing dynastic prospects—Tiberius' son Drusus (see no. **21** above) and the children of Germanicus and the elder Agrippina (Tac. *Ann.* 4. 12). If Tacitus is accurate with his *neque senatorio ambitu abstinebat* etc. (and there is no good reason to doubt him), Sejanus' influence over Tiberius, and the degree to which he was privy to affairs of state, were now dangerously great. Yet he was no more than an equestrian.

These developments, including the public honours conferred on Sejanus, took place at the same time as changes in the type-content of the *aes* coinage struck at Rome (the types of the gold and silver, struck at Lugdunum, were unchanged throughout virtually the whole reign: see no. 9 above). That *aes* had begun in AD 15–16 with the uninformative (?)'Livia' type for Tiberius (*RIC* I², p. 96, nos. 33–6) and the first of the 'Divus Augustus' issues (ibid., p. 99, nos. 71–3). Probably *c.*AD 22 the conspicuous *Clementiae* and *Moderationi* dupondii appeared (see no. **23** below)—the first Roman imperial coins to express publicly a 'value-judgement' upon a reigning *princeps*, and doing so by means of quite unprecedented types. These were followed in AD 22–3 (Tiberius as *tr.pot. XXIIII*; for the validity of 22–3 for the coins see Sutherland, *CRIP*, pp. 191 ff.) by *aes* coin-issues alluding emphatically to *Iustitia*, *Pietas*, and *Salus* (see *b*, *c*, and *d*) together with types in honour of Drusus (*a*),

Livia, Divus Augustus, and the twin boys born to Drusus' wife
Livilla in AD 19 (Tac. *Ann.* 2. 84) (*RIC* I², p. 97, nos. 42–51).

It is legitimate to argue the extent to which imperial coin-
types were intended for public information or persuasion (see
most recently Barbara Levick in *Antichthon* 16 (1982),
pp. 104 ff.; Sutherland in *NACQT* 1983, pp. 151 ff., and *Rev.
Num.* 1983, pp. 73 ff.), but it would not be legitimate to deny
that AD 22–3 saw a complete change in the idiom, and thus
probably the direction, of the types of the *aes* of Rome. On
the one hand it has been held (cf. Sutherland, *CRIP*,
pp. 91 ff.) that Sejanus, ambitious to succeed Tiberius (who,
as only the second *princeps*, was now in his mid-sixties; cf.
Suet. *Tib.* 5), and determined to destroy Tiberius' dynastic
plans (Tac. *Ann.* 4. 3 f.), decided to publicize the virtuous and
favourable qualities of Tiberius' principate as a preliminary to
his own plotted succession. In this he could well have been
helped by the influence which, as Tacitus records, he was
able to exert over his social and political superiors, as a result
of which he could have manipulated the choice of coin-types
at the mint of Rome. On the other hand there is the view (cf.
Woodman, *Velleius Paterculus . . .*, pp. 245 ff.) that Sejanus was
in a true sense Tiberius' *principalium onerum adiutor* (Vell. Pat.
2. 127. 3), *socius laborum* (Tac. *Ann.* 4. 2), *adiutor imperii* (Tac.
Ann. 4. 7), and σύμβουλος καὶ ὑπηρέτης πρὸς πάντα (Dio Cass.
57. 19. 7). This view, however, fails to explain the obvious
discrepancy between Sejanus as Tiberius' *adiutor* and Sejanus
as the proven destroyer of Tiberius' dynastic plans, a discrepancy explicable only (it would seem) if Sejanus was a false
adiutor.

One thing alone can be surely demonstrated. When Tiberius resumed a systematic *aes* coinage at Rome from AD 34 to
37 (*RIC* I², pp. 97 f., nos. 52–69), the types employed, while
showing an obvious advance upon those of Augustus in
regard to idiom and design, were much more restrained than
those of AD 22–3, the innovations of which were now quite
abandoned.

23. *Moderatio* and *Clementia* under Tiberius

1. Tac. *Ann.* 3. 51. Id (i.e. the hasty execution of Clutorius Priscus in AD 21) Tiberius solitis sibi ambagibus apud senatum incusavit, cum extolleret pietatem quamvis modicas principis iniurias acriter ulciscentium, deprecaretur tam praecipitis verborum poenas.

2. Tac. *Ann.* 3. 56. Tiberius, fama moderationis parta quod ingruentis accusatores represserat . . . (of AD 22).

Suet. *Tib.* 32. 2. Parem moderationem minoribus quoque et personis et rebus exhibuit . . . Praesidibus onerandas tributo provincias suadentibus rescripsit boni pastoris esse tondere pecus, non deglubere.

4. Seneca, *De Clem.* 1. 2. Clementiam quamvis poena digni invocent, etiam innocentes colunt . . . Itaque adhibenda moderatio est, quae sanabilia ingenia distinguere a deploratis sciat . . . Modum tenere debemus.

Id. 1. 9. Divus Augustus fuit mitis princeps.

Id. 1. 11. Clementiam non voco lassam crudelitatem: haec est, Caesar, clementia vera . . . nullam habere maculam, numquam civilem sanguinem fudisse.

Tac. *Ann.* 3. 51. Tiberius criticized this in the senate with his usual ambiguity. He praised the senate's sense of duty in avenging even small slights against the emperor, but deprecated such hasty punishment of mere words.

Tac. *Ann.* 3. 56. Tiberius had gained credit for moderation by checking the growing power of the informers.

Suet. *Tib.* 32. 2. He showed the same sense of moderation in lesser concerns too, both personal and otherwise . . . When provincial authorities urged him to increase provincial tribute, he wrote back saying that a good shepherd should shear his flock, not flay it.

Seneca, *De Clem.* 1. 2. Though men who deserve punishment call on clemency, it is the innocent who worship it . . . And so moderation must be applied, for it knows how to distinguish between the curable and the completely abandoned characters.

Id. 1. 9. Divus Augustus was a gentle princeps.

Id. 1. 11. I do not call clemency a condition of exhausted cruelty. True clemency, Sir, consists in this—to be without blemish, never to have shed the blood of citizens.

23a   23b

a RIC I², p. 97, no. 38. Dupondius of Rome, *c.*AD 16–22. *Obv.*
TI(*berius*) CAESAR DIVI AVG(*usti*) F(*ilius*) AVGVST(*us*)
IMP(*erator*) VIII, Head of Tiberius, laureate. *Rev.* CLEMEN-
TIAE, S C, Small facing bust within laurel-wreath on ornamental
round shield within outer circle of palmettes and dots.

b RIC I², p. 97, nos. 39f. Dupondius of Rome, *c.*AD 16–22. *Obv.* As
last. *Rev.* MODERATIONI (very rarely MODERATIONIS),
S C, Small facing bust in ornamental border within foliate and
dotted outer circle.

Clementia had openly emerged as a primary imperial quality
under Augustus, being publicly acknowledged in the presentation of the golden shield *virtutis clementiaeque iustitiae et pietatis
caussa* to Augustus (*RG* 34. 2; see no. 4 above); and both
clementia, a favourable disposition of mind in the infliction of
punishment, and *moderatio*, limitation of the penalty incurred,
had been qualities attributed earlier to Julius Caesar (Suet.
Div. Iul. 75. 1). Augustus' *virtus* and *moderatio* were factors in
attracting the *amicitia* of foreign peoples with Rome (Suet. *Div.
Aug.* 21. 3), and his *clementia* was later to be held up as an
example to the young Nero upon his accession (Seneca, *De
Clem.* 1. 10. 3). If Tiberius wished, even privately, to emulate

the primary imperial qualities of Augustus—though he publicly professed that to be impossible (Tac. *Ann.* 1. 11)—he knew that his *virtus* was assured by his eminent military record under Augustus (see no. 10 above), while his *pietas* was amply attested by the honours which he paid to Divus Augustus (see no. 15). And in AD 22–3 dupondii from the mint of Rome (*RIC* I², p. 97, no. 46) conspicuously emphasized *iustitia* (see above, no. 22*c*), though the exact reason for this coinage-issue is not clear.

Earlier, however, at some date within the period AD 16–22 (Tiberius as IMP VIII), the mint of Rome issued a double (because die-linked; Sutherland, *JRS* 1938, pp. 129 ff.) series of dupondii celebrating *clementia* and *moderatio*, each of these types showing a small, decorated *imago clupeata* bearing a facing bust in the manner seen under Augustus (*RIC* I², p. 68, no. 356). Various attempts have been made to identify these little busts, sometimes at the cost of assigning the coins which bear them to a stylistically very improbable date (cf. *Num. Chron.* 1979, pp. 21 ff.), as was also done, though on different grounds, by Grant (*RAI*, pp. 47 ff., on which see Sutherland, *CRIP*, pp. 191 ff.). It is Tacitus who appears to give the clue to the date of Tiberius' die-linked *clementiae* and *moderationi* dupondii. In a passing and clearly annalistic phrase in the ablative absolute, quite unconnected with the main and finite sentence with which *Ann.* 3. 56 begins, he attributes the credit which Tiberius gained for *moderatio* to his check (in AD 22) to state informers, even though he did not entirely suppress them: such limitation was the essence of *moderatio*. One year earlier, in the affair of the imprudent Clutorius Priscus (Tac. *Ann.* 3. 49–51; cf. Dio Cass. 57. 20. 3–4), who had allowed his poetic muse to anticipate Drusus' death, Tiberius had ordered an automatic nine-day stay of execution before sentences of death should be carried out. In neither instance is Tacitus' treatment of Tiberius' action at all generous; but Tiberius himself, as well as the senate, could have considered them praiseworthy. The senate may therefore have decided to present him with *clupei* to mark his *clementia* and *moderatio*; and coins commemorating their honorific action could thus have been produced in AD 22.

24. The 'financial crisis' of AD 33

1. Tac. *Ann.* 6. 17. Hinc inopia rei nummariae, commoto simul omnium aere alieno, et quia tot damnatis bonisque eorum divenditis signatum argentum fisco vel aerario attinebatur. Ad hoc senatus praescripserat, duas quisque faenoris partis in agris per Italiam conlocaret. Sed creditores in solidum appellabant ... multique fortunis provolvebantur ... donec tulit opem Caesar disposito per mensas milies sestertio factaque mutuandi copia sine usuris per triennium (of AD 33).

2. Suet. *Tib.* 48. 1. Publice munificentiam bis omnino exhibuit ... quorum alterum magna difficultate nummaria populo auxilium flagitante coactus est facere, cum per senatus consultum sanxisset, ut faeneratores duas patrimonii partes in solo collocarent, debitores totidem aeris alieni statim solverent, nec res expediretur.

3. Dio Cass. 58. 21. 5. τό τε πρᾶγμα τὸ κατὰ τὰ δανείσματα ἐμετρίασε, καὶ δισχιλίας καὶ πεντακοσίας μυριάδας τῷ δημοσίῳ ἔδωκεν ὥστ᾽ αὐτὰς ὑπ᾽ ἀνδρῶν βουλευτῶν ἀτοκεὶ τοῖς δεομένοις ἐς τρία ἔτη ἐκδανεισθῆναι.

Tac. *Ann.* 6. 17. From this arose a scarcity of coinage, as credit everywhere had been upset and silver coinage was immobilized in the imperial or the public treasury through the conviction of so many persons and the sale of their assets. To meet this difficulty the senate had directed that every creditor should secure two-thirds of his capital on land in Italy. But creditors were calling for payment in full ... Many lost their whole fortune ... until the emperor came to the rescue by distributing 100 million sesterces through the banks and by allowing interest-free loans for a three-year period.

Suet. *Tib.* 48. 1. He (Tiberius) twice showed public generosity ... In one instance there was a great currency crisis, and the people called urgently for help, so that, after he had regularized procedure by a decree of the senate, he laid it down that creditors should invest two-thirds of their personal fortune in land, and that debtors should at once pay the same proportion of their indebtedness.

Dio Cass. 58. 21. 5. Tiberius modified his decision regarding loans, giving 25 million denarii to the public treasury so that interest-free loans could be made by the senate from this sum for a three-year period to those who needed them.

The 'shortage of money' in AD 33, which was a matter of the circulation of coinage and not of its supply (see in general Rodewald, *MAT*, especially pp. 1 ff., 70 f.; review by E. Lo Cascio in *JRS* 1978, pp. 201 f., with further discussion in *JRS*

1981, p. 85; for the problem of debt see M. W. Fredericksen in *JRS* 1966, pp. 132 f.), was caused by the sudden and widespread prosecution (Tac. *Ann.* 6. 16) of those—including many senators—who had infringed Julius Caesar's legislation on usury by securing a major part of their capital on Italian estates. Tiberius, to whom the problem was referred, granted an eighteen-month period of grace to allow the legal requirements to be met. In consequence, much mortgaged land had to be sold, and coinage (Tacitus specified silver coinage) became locked up and immobilized in the public *aerarium* or the imperial *fiscus*. This, in a free market economy based on supply and demand, caused the *inopia* of current coin, a shortage which would, in turn, have tended to increase commodity prices in Rome and Italy, already a matter of concern a decade earlier (Tac. *Ann.* 3. 52, *vetita . . . utensilium pretia augeri in dies*) when Tiberius himself deplored the outflow of imperial coinage across the Roman frontiers in exchange for the import of exotic luxury goods (Tac. *Ann.* 3. 53). Faced with the *inopia* of AD 33 Tiberius reacted quickly and sensibly, and without any recorded need to turn bullion into additional coinage. He simply freed 100 million sesterces (or more probably, in view of Tacitus' *argentum signatum* and of Dio Cassius' account, 25 million denarii) for circulation in the money-market through the *mensarii*, the bankers of the day.

No great flood of newly coined money is therefore discernible in, or even after, AD 33. It would be virtually impossible to detect any such thing at Lugdunum, where the aurei and denarii were now always undated; and no gold or silver was ever issued for Tiberius at Rome. Rome, however, did resume a regular, fairly abundant, and dated series of *aes* sestertii and asses from AD 34–5 until his death (*RIC* I², pp. 97 f., nos. 52–69), this resumption of regular *aes* presumably acting as a token-coinage counterbalance for an increased circulation of silver.

25. Tiberius and the *corona civica*

1. Suet. *Tib.* 26. 2. Praenomen quoque imperatoris cognomenque patris patriae et civicam in vestibulo coronam recusavit (Tiberius); ac ne Augusti quidem nomen, quanquam hereditarium, ullis nisi ad reges ac dynastas epistulis addidit.

2. Dio Cass. 57. 2. 1. ἔς τε τὰ στρατόπεδα καὶ ἐς τὰ ἔθνη πάντα ὡς αὐτοκράτωρ εὐθὺς ἀπὸ τῆς Νώλης ἐπέστειλε, μὴ λέγων αὐτοκράτωρ εἶναι· ψηφισθὲν γάρ αὐτῷ καὶ τοῦτο μετὰ τῶν ἄλλων ὀνομάτων οὐκ ἐδέξατο, καὶ τὸν κλῆρον τοῦ Αὐγούστου λαβὼν τὴν ἐπίκλησιν αὐτοῦ ταύτην οὐκ ἔθετο (of AD 14).

3. Tac. *Ann.* 3. 21. Quo proelio (against Tacfarinas' troops) Rufus Helvius gregarius miles servati civis decus rettulit donatusque est ab Apronio torquibus et hasta. Caesar addidit civicam coronam, quod non eam quoque Apronius iure proconsulis tribuisset questus magis quam offensus (of AD 20).

Suet. *Tib.* 26. 2. Tiberius also declined the forename of 'Imperator', as well as the added style of 'Father of his Country' and the civic crown at his entrance-hall. And he did not even add the name 'Augustus' (though it was his by inheritance) in any official letters except those to client kings and local dynasts.

Dio Cass. 57. 2. 1. Tiberius wrote at once from Nola (i.e. after Augustus' death) to the army camps and to the provinces as *imperator*, though not saying that he was in fact *imperator*. This title was indeed voted to him along with others, but he did not accept it; and though he took the inheritance left him by Augustus, he did not take the appellation 'Augustus' either.

Tac. *Ann.* 3. 21. In that battle Helvius Rufus, an ordinary soldier, won the distinction of saving a fellow citizen's life, and Apronius presented him with armlets and a spear. Tiberius added the civic crown, complaining (though without anger) that Apronius, as proconsul, could have done this by right.

25a

a RIC I², p. 99, no. 79. Dupondius of Rome. *c.*AD 22–6. *Obv.* DIVVS AVGVSTVS PATER, Head of Augustus, with radiate crown. *Rev.* S C in oak-wreath.

b RIC I², p. 98, no. 57. Sestertius of Rome, AD 34–5. *Obv.* DIVO

AVGVSTO S P Q R, Shield inscribed OB CIVES SER(*vatos*) in oak-wreath supported by capricorns above globe. *Rev.* TI(*berius*) CAESAR DIVI AVG(*usti*) F(*ilius*) AVGVST(*us*) P(*ontifex*) M(*aximus*) TR(*ibunicia*) POT(*estate*) XXXVI around S C (cf. no. **15**f.).

c   *RIC* I², p. 99, no. 70. Sestertius(?) of Rome, *c*.AD 15–16. *Obv.* DIVVS AVGVSTVS PATER, Head of Augustus, with radiate crown, star, and thunderbolt. *Rev.* No legend. Head of Tiberius surrounded by oak-wreath.

The civic crown of oak-leaves *ob cives servatos* (on which see S. Weinstock, *DI*, p. 163) voted to Augustus by the senate on 13 January 27 BC (*RG* 34. 2; *Fast. Praen.* under this date; cf. Dio Cass. 53. 16. 4; W. K. Lacey in *JRS* 1974, pp. 177 f.) was among the most prominent of all elements in the wide range of Augustus' coin-types, being standard on the *aes* of Rome from *c*.18 to 6 BC (*RIC* I², pp. 65–76), and appearing also in the types of the aurei and denarii of Rome and of the 'uncertain mints of Spain' (*RIC* I², pp. 43 ff., 62 ff.), and in the *aes* of an unidentified (?)eastern mint (*RIC* I², p. 86, nos. 549 f.). It was also a conspicuous feature in the decoration of the great altar shown on the abundant *aes* of Lugdunum (*RIC* I², p. 57, nos. 229 f.). After Augustus' death Tiberius continually emphasized his predecessor's *corona civica* on the *aes* of Rome until the end of his own principate (see *a* and *b*; also no. **15** f. above), but according to Suetonius and Dio Cassius he declined the *corona civica* for himself: his argument would probably have been that, whereas Augustus had rescued the state and its citizens from civil war, he himself had done no more as emperor than to succeed Augustus. The same sources record that he also declined the *praenomen* 'imperator', as well as the styles *pater patriae* and *Augustus*.

His coinage, indeed, never shows the *praenomen imperatoris*, or the style *pater patriae*; but on the coins both of Rome and of Lugdunum he was styled Augustus with absolute regularity (see here Seager, *Tiberius*, p. 143). With one possible exception—a very rare and conceivably medallic (because abnormally heavy) *aes* issue of AD 15–16 (see *c*)—the *corona civica* never appeared as a personal attribute on Tiberius' coinage, thus confirming Suetonius' statement. Perhaps characteristically, however, while declining for himself what his successors automatically accepted (on the ground that by their accession they had saved the body politic from rival dissensions), Tiberius took care that the merit of a common soldier for an act of bravery in the African war against Tacfarinas should not be overlooked. That soldier's bravery constituted, even now, the strict justification for the award of the *corona civica*.

26. Gaius and the deification of Tiberius

1. Suet. *C. Calig.* 15. 1. Incendebat et ipse studia hominum omni genere popularitatis. Tiberio cum plurimis lacrimis pro contione laudato funeratoque amplissime, confestim Pandateriam ... festinavit.

2. Dio Cass. 59. 3. 7. τόν τε Τιβέριον αὐτόν, ὃν καὶ πάππον προσωνόμαζε, τῶν αὐτῶν τῷ Αὐγούστῳ τιμῶν παρὰ τῆς βουλῆς τυχεῖν ἀξιώσας, ἔπειτ' ἐπειδὴ μὴ παραχρῆμα ἐψηφίσθησαν (οὔτε γὰρ τιμῆσαι αὐτὸν ὑπομένοντες οὔτ' ἀτιμάσαι θαρσοῦντες, ἅτε μηδέπω τὴν τοῦ νεανίσκου γνώμην σαφῶς εἰδότες, ἐς τὴν παρουσίαν αὐτοῦ πάντα ἀνεβάλλοντο), οὐδενὶ ἄλλῳ πλὴν τῇ δημοσίᾳ ταφῇ ἤγηλε, νυκτός τε ἐς τὴν πόλιν τὸ σῶμα αὐτοῦ ἐσαγαγὼν καὶ ἅμα τῇ ἕῳ προθέμενος. ἐποιήσατο μὲν γὰρ καὶ λόγους ἐπ' αὐτῷ, ἀλλ' οὔτι γε καὶ ἐκεῖνον οὕτως ἐπαινῶν ὡς τοῦ τε Αὐγούστου καὶ τοῦ Γερμανικοῦ τὸν δῆμον ἀναμιμνήσκων, καὶ ἑαυτὸν αὐτοῖς παρακατατιθέμενος (of AD 37).

Suet. *C. Calig.* 15. 1. Gaius himself set about firing people's enthusiasm by courting popularity in all kinds of ways. He praised Tiberius, very tearfully, at a public meeting, and furnished an elaborate funeral for him. Then he hurried off, without any delay, to Pandateria.

Dio Cass. 59. 3. 7. Gaius thought it right that Tiberius (whom he called grandfather) should receive the same honours from the senate as Augustus had received. But in the event the senators had failed to vote for this at once, for they could neither bring themselves to honour him nor have the courage to dishonour him, having no clear knowledge of the young man's mind, and so they deferred everything until he should be present. So Gaius bestowed upon him nothing more than public burial, after bringing the body into Rome by night and displaying it around dawn. He made an oration over it, not however so much by way of praising Tiberius as of recalling Augustus and Germanicus and pledging himself to their standards.

26a **26b**

a *BMCRE* I, p. 146, no. 1, with pl. 27, 1. Aureus of Lugdunum, AD 37–8. *Obv.* C(*aius*) CAESAR AVG(*ustus*) GERM(*anicus*) P(*ontifex*) M(*aximus*) TR(*ibunicia*) POT(*estate*) COS, Head of Gaius, bare. *Rev.* No legend. Head, with features of Tiberius, wearing radiate crown, between two stars.

b *RIC* I², p. 108, no. 2. Denarius of Lugdunum, AD 37–8. As last coin, but the *rev.* head with the features of Augustus.

c *RIC* I², p. 108, no. 3. Aureus of Lugdunum, AD 37–8. *Obv.* C(*aius*) CAESAR AVG(*ustus*) GERM(*anicus*) P(*ontifex*) M(*aximus*) TR(*ibunicia*) POT(*estate*), Head of Gaius, bare. *Rev.* DIVVS AVG(*ustus*) PATER PATRIAE, Head with the features of Augustus; no stars.

The loss of Tacitus' *Annals* books 7–10 deprives us of what would have been a detailed account of the events following immediately after Tiberius' death in his seventy-eighth year, hastened, according to Suetonius (*Tib.* 73. 2; *C. Calig.* 12. 2 f.), on Gaius' behalf by Macro. Tiberius' recently made will had named Gaius (now 25 years old) as equal co-heir with another and younger grandson, Drusus' son Tiberius (Suet. *Tib.* 76). No question arose of the younger co-heir's right of succession to Tiberius, and it was not long before he was put to death, though he had first been made *princeps iuventutis* (Suet. *C. Calig.* 15. 3; 23. 3), a step doubtless taken to show that his disqualifying youth (cf. Dio Cass. 59. 1. 2) relegated him to the next generation of succession. The young Gaius received a warm welcome to imperial power, and this warmth extended to the conspicuous *pietas* which he showed towards the members of his own family, both dead (Suet. *C. Calig.* 15) and alive (see below, no. **29**). Some degree of *pietas* was shown also to the dead Tiberius, according to Suetonius. Dio Cassius goes further, implying Gaius' initial intention of conferring on Tiberius 'the same honours as were paid to Augustus' (i.e. including consecration)—an intention which quickly lapsed in consequence of the senate's ambivalence in the face of the young emperor's failure to give a lead.

This oddly confused situation may have been due to Gaius' wish to do two things, first, to provide himself with all the available constitutional props, including Tiberius' deification with the post-mortem rituals on the pattern of those accorded to Augustus, and secondly to consolidate his own strong initial popularity by distancing himself as much as possible from his unpopular predecessor (see the discussion in Balsdon, *Gaius*, pp. 24–9). And it may possibly account for the fact that a few of the earliest aurei and denarii of Gaius' principate (only four obverse and four reverse dies have been recorded; cf. J.-B. Giard in *Rev. Num.* 1976, p. 73) bear a reverse type (see *a*) which appears to portray an idealized head of the aged Tiberius between two stars, and wearing the radiate crown of divinity—all without explanatory legend—rather than the clearly Augustan features, also radiate, at first with stars but without legend, which followed (see *b* and *c*). All of these early coins of Gaius were struck at Lugdunum, where Tiberius' long series of gold and silver had also been coined (see no. **9** above; *RIC* I², pp. 87 ff., 102 f.), and the Lugdunum mint could well have assumed that Tiberius' death would be followed automatically by his deification. Equally possibly, Gaius' first intention to deify could have been instantly sent off by official messengers (cf. the flood of dispatches sent off by Tiberius himself in AD 14; Dio Cass. 57. 2. 1) and not immediately countermanded. Any such view obviously depends upon the subjective ground of the recognition of Tiberian as distinct from Augustan features on the coins in question. But there are the other and visible elements to be assessed: absence of reverse legend followed by the ultimate DIVVS AVGVSTVS PATER, and the two stars (for two *divi*?) followed by the absence of stars. These plainly visible changes would seem to underline the significance of variable portraiture.

27. Gaius and the Praetorians

1. Dio Cass. 59. 2. 1. πρὸς δὲ τὰ καταλειφθέντα ὑπ᾽ αὐτοῦ (i.e.
Tiberius) πάντα, ὡς καὶ παρ᾽ ἑαυτοῦ δή, τοῖς τε ἄλλοις ἀποδοὺς μεγαλο-
ψυχίας τινὰ δόξαν παρὰ τοῖς πολλοῖς ἐκτήσατο. τούς τε οὖν δορυφόρους
εὐθὺς γυμνασίαν ποιουμένους θεασάμενος μετὰ τῆς γερουσίας, τάς τε
καταλειφθείσας σφίσι κατὰ πεντήκοντα καὶ διακοσίας δραχμὰς διένειμε
καὶ ἑτέρας τοσαύτας προσεπέδωκε (of AD 37).

Dio Cass. 59. 2. 1. Gaius paid out all Tiberius' bequests as if they
were his own, and gained a general reputation for magnanimity.
Thus he held a parade of the Praetorians, whom he reviewed in the
presence of the senate, and distributed the 250 denarii per man
bequeathed to them, with as much again as a gift from himself.

27a

a RIC I², p. 110, no. 32. Sestertius of Rome, AD 37–8. *Obv.* C(*aius*)
CAESAR AVG(*ustus*) GERMANICVS PON(*tifex*) M(*aximus*)
TR(*ibunicia*) POT(*estate*), Head of Gaius, laureate. *Rev.*
ADLOCVT(*io*) COH(*ortium*), Gaius, togate, standing on plat-
form, extending his hand to five armed soldiers, of whom each
soldier in the two rearmost pairs carries an *aquila*.

The provisions of Tiberius' will were cancelled after Gaius'
accession (Suet. *C. Calig.* 16. 3), but Gaius, with obvious
prudence, did not allow this to affect the distribution to the
Praetorians of the money left to them among Tiberius' other
military legacies (cf. Suet. *Tib.* 76; Balsdon, *Gaius*, pp. 182f.).
A special review of the Praetorians in AD 37, presumably soon
after Tiberius' death (cf. Dio Cass. 59. 1 and the εὐθύς of 59. 2.
1), was the occasion for this distribution. The sum previously
bequeathed by Augustus to the Praetorians had been 1,000 sestertii per man (Tac. *Ann.* 1. 8), and Tiberius had repeated that

same figure, correctly expressed by Dio Cassius as 250 denarii. To pay each man 1,000 actual brass sestertii would have been extremely cumbrous and difficult—a weight of some 60 lb. per man. Payment in denarii would have been much easier—some 8 lb. per man. Ten aurei, weighing some 6 ounces, would have been easier still. It may be the case, however, that Gaius paid Tiberius' legacy at least partly in the form of *aes* sestertii. A single aureus was worth 100 sestertii, and a half-aureus 50, and it is worth noting that half-aurei were coined for Gaius in AD 37, 38–9, and 40–1 (*RIC* I^2, pp. 108f., nos. 5, 20, and 29) and that *Adlocut*(io) *Coh*(ortium) sestertii ('Cohortium' in the plural because the parading soldiers carry no less than four standards) were coined in AD 37–8, 39–40, and 40–1 (*RIC* I^2, pp. 110f., nos. 32, 40, and 48). Tiberius' bequest of 1,000 sestertii per man could have been conveniently paid in the combination of 9$\frac{1}{2}$ aurei, 12 denarii, and 2 of these fine, quasi-medallic sestertii—a weight of less than 1$\frac{1}{2}$ lb. per man. Gaius' decision to double Tiberius' bequest on his own account (presumably a reflection of his sense of their military and political importance, on which see Campbell, *ERA*, pp. 109–20) would have meant a weight of some 3 lb. in all.

The issue of the *Adlocut Coh* sestertii in AD 39–40 and 40–1 raises the possibility that Gaius distributed largesse to the Praetorians after AD 37. A conspicuous feature of all these splendid *Adlocut Coh* sestertii is the absence from them of the formula S C which had been normal on all *aes* since Augustus except for that marked S P Q R, in which S C is subsumed (cf. *RIC* I^2, pp. 96f., nos. 11f.; p. 112, no. 55). If it is correct to conclude that it was the senate which authorized the withdrawal from the *aerarium* of *aes* for coinage (see no. 14 above), these sestertii of Gaius without S C promote the further conclusion that Gaius, for these particular coin-issues, authorized the withdrawal of *aes* by the simple exercise of his *arbitrium*, so enthusiastically accorded to the *exoptatissimus princeps* during the heady period of his accession (Suet. *C. Calig.* 13. 1; 14. 1). His later and unconcealed scorn of the senate (Suet. *C. Calig.* 26. 2) would equally have enabled him to authorize withdrawal of *aes*, against the normal convention, in AD 39–40 and 40–1.

28. The title *Pater Patriae* and the *corona civica* under Gaius

1. Dio Cass. 59. 3. 1 f. τῷ δ᾽ αὐτῷ τούτῳ τρόπῳ καὶ ἐς τἆλλα πάντα ὡς εἰπεῖν ἐχρῆτο. δημοκρατικώτατός τε γὰρ εἶναι τὰ πρῶτα δόξας, ὥστε μήτε τῷ δήμῳ ἢ τῇ γε βουλῇ γράψαι τι μήτε τῶν ὀνομάτων τῶν ἀρχικῶν προσθέσθαι τι, μοναρχικώτατος ἐγένετο, ὥστε πάντα ὅσα ὁ Αὔγουστος ἐν τοσούτῳ τῆς ἀρχῆς χρόνῳ μόλις καὶ καθ᾽ ἓν ἕκαστον ψηφισθέντα οἱ ἐδέξατο, ὧν ἔνια ὁ Τιβέριος οὐδ᾽ ὅλως προσήκατο, ἐν μιᾷ ἡμέρᾳ λαβεῖν. πλὴν γὰρ τῆς τοῦ πατρὸς ἐπικλήσεως οὐδὲν ἄλλο ἀνεβάλετο· καὶ ἐκείνην δὲ οὐκ ἐς μακρὰν προσεκτήσατο.

Dio Cass. 59. 3. 1 f. In all other matters too the same deterioration was generally the case. At first he had seemed the most democratic of men, to the extent, indeed, that he would send nothing in writing either to the people or to the senate, and would assume none of the imperial titles. Then he became very royal, and in one day accepted all the honours which, voted over a long reign, Augustus had accepted one by one, and reluctantly. Some of these, indeed, Tiberius had altogether refused. But Gaius deferred none of them except the title *Pater* (*Patriae*), and he acquired even that before long.

28a

a *RIC* I², p. 109, no. 13. Aureus of Rome, AD 37–8. *Obv.* C(*aius*) CAESAR AVG(*ustus*) GERM(*anicus*) P(*ontifex*) M(*aximus*) TR(*ibunicia*) POT(*estate*), Head of Gaius, laureate. *Rev.* AGRIPPINA MAT(*er*) C(*ai*) CAES(*aris*) AVG(*usti*) GERM(*anici*), Bust of Agrippina the Elder.

b *RIC* I², p. 109, no. 19. Denarius of Rome, AD 37–8. *Obv.* As *a. Rev.* S P Q R P(*ater*) P(*atriae*) OB C(*ives*) S(*ervatos*) in oak-wreath.

c *RIC* I², p. 111, no. 47. As of Rome, AD 39–40. *Obv.* C(*aius*) CAESAR DIVI AVG(*usti*) PRON(*epos*) AVG(*ustus*) P(*ontifex*) M(*aximus*) TR(*ibunicia*) P(*otestate*) III P(*ater*) P(*atriae*), Head of Gaius, bare. *Rev.* VESTA, S C, Vesta, seated, holding patera and sceptre.

Dio Cassius records Gaius' acceptance, after his accession, of a parcel of honours simultaneously conferred 'in one day'. Gaius' coinage shows (cf. *a–c*) that, like Claudius (Suet. *Div. Claud.* 12. 1), he never adopted the *praenomen imperatoris* (cf. Balsdon, *Gaius*, p. 146), but his attitude with regard to the title *pater patriae* (never accepted by Tiberius; cf. Suet. *Tib.* 26. 2) is less clear. According to Dio Cassius he deferred it for a short time—again like Claudius—and then assumed it, as coins of AD 37–8 testify, together with the *corona civica* (see *b*). Tiberius had refused the *corona civica* (see no. **25** above), but from Gaius' time onward it declared that an emperor's assumption of power had saved the body-politic (cf. *RIC* I², pp. 122ff., 241, 245ff., 272ff.).

The title P(*ater*) P(*atriae*), however, was never included in the formal titulature of Gaius' aurei and denarii at any time in his reign, and appeared on *aes* only in AD 39–41 (see *c*). *Aes* of Gaius, like his gold and silver (see *b*), show the *corona civica* of oak-leaves from 37 onwards; but Gaius' erratic estimate of this honour is perhaps suggested by Suetonius' account (*C. Calig.* 19. 2) of his riding on a decorated horse along the bridge of Baiae, 'resplendent ... with a crown of oak-leaves, buckler, sword, and golden cloak'. According to Weinstock (*DI*, pp. 280f.) he even displayed the *corona civica* on a *fastigium* on his palace. By contrast, Tiberius had taken a strictly proper view of the honorific quality (cf. Gellius 5. 6. 1) of the *corona civica* (see no. **25** above).

The attribution to the mint of Rome of the aurei and denarii of Gaius described in *a* and *b* above is in accordance with the view followed in *RIC* I², pp. 102ff. (cf. also Sutherland, *The Emperor and the Coinage*, pp. 64ff.), against that of J.-B. Giard (*Rev. Num.* 1976, pp. 69ff.), who attributes the whole of Gaius' gold and silver coinage to Lugdunum.

29. Gaius and his three sisters

1. Suet. *C. Calig.* 15. 3. De sororibus auctor fuit, ut omnibus sacramentis adiceretur 'neque me liberosque meos cariores habebo quam Gaium habeo et sorores eius', item relationibus consulum 'quod bonum felixque sit C. Caesari sororibusque eius'.

2. Dio Cass. 59. 3. 4. καὶ ταῖς ἀδελφαῖς ταῦτά τε τὰ τῶν ἀειπαρθένων καὶ τὸ τὰς ἱπποδρομίας οἵ ἐν τῇ αὐτῇ προεδρίᾳ συνθεᾶσθαι, τό τε τάς τε εὐχὰς τὰς κατ᾽ ἔτος ὑπὸ τῶν ἀρχόντων καὶ ὑπὸ τῶν ἱερέων ὑπέρ τε ἑαυτοῦ καὶ ὑπὲρ τοῦ δημοσίου ποιουμένας καὶ τοὺς ὅρκους τοὺς ἐς τὴν ἀρχὴν αὐτοῦ φέροντας καὶ ὑπὲρ ἐκείνων ὁμοίως γίγνεσθαι ἔνειμε (of AD 37).

Suet. *C. Calig.* 15. 3. He was responsible for the inclusion of his sisters' names in all oaths, in the form 'I shall not hold myself or my children dearer than I hold Gaius and his sisters'. Similarly, formal consular motions included the words 'wishing favour and happiness to Gaius Caesar and his sisters'.

Dio Cass. 59. 3. 4. To his sisters Gaius gave the privileges of Vestal Virgins, and the right of watching the games in the Circus from seats in his own enclosure. And annual vows made by the magistrates and priests for his own well-being and that of the state were now to include his sisters, who were also to share in the oaths of allegiance sworn to the imperial regime.

29a

a RIC I², p. 110, no. 33. Sestertius of Rome, AD 37–8. *Obv.* C(*aius*) CAESAR AVG(*ustus*) GERMANICVS PON(*tifex*) M(*aximus*) TR(*ibunicia*) POT(*estate*), Head of Gaius, laureate. *Rev.* AGRIPPINA DRVSILLA IVLIA, S C, Gaius' three sisters standing facing; Agrippina as Securitas, resting on column and with cornucopia; Drusilla as Concordia, with patera and cornucopia; and Julia as Fortuna, with rudder and cornucopia.

After the death of Augustus senatorial efforts were made to have conspicuous honours conferred on his widow Livia: she should be styled *parens* or *mater patriae*, and Tiberius should be named *Iuliae filius* (Tac. *Ann.* 1. 14). Tiberius opposed the voting of any such honours to women, and the suggestions were dropped, though the *feriae* of 17 January, commemorating Octavian's marriage with Livia in 38 BC, may now have been instituted (cf. Gagé on *RG*, p. 166). Even when Livia herself died in AD 29 Tiberius refused to allow the deification of this great imperial lady (Vell. Pat. 130. 5; Tac. *Ann.* 5. 2 commented that Livia would have agreed with his decision). The young Gaius, upon his accession, showed a very different attitude in respect of his three sisters, Agrippina, Drusilla, and Julia, now 22, 21, and 20 years old respectively, as Suetonius and Dio Cassius carefully explain.

Gaius' aurei and denarii from AD 37 onwards witnessed his emphasis on family unity (cf. *RIC* I², pp. 108 ff.) with their commemorative portraits of his father and mother, the renowned Germanicus and elder Agrippina. This emphasis was underlined by his affection for his sisters (unnaturally great, according to some rumour; Suet. *C. Calig.* 24. 1), which prompted the fine and remarkable sestertii struck at Rome in AD 37–8 and again (*RIC* I², p. 111, no. 41) in 39(–40). Drusilla in fact died in 38, after which any mention of her on coinage was plainly commemorative: she became the object of various cults (cf. Smallwood, *Documents. . . Gaius–Nero*, nos. 5, 11, 128, 401). Agrippina and Julia were both exiled, on suspicion of treason, in 39 (cf. Suet. *C. Calig.* 24. 3), so that no 'three sisters' coins appeared thereafter. No such prominence was to be accorded to living imperial ladies for over a decade to come, until Claudius produced gold and silver in honour of this same younger Agrippina between AD 50 and 54 (*RIC* I², pp. 125 f., nos. 75, 80). She was to be further honoured on coinage in 55 by her son, the young Nero, shortly after his accession (*RIC* I², p. 150, nos. 6 f.; cf. no. 35 below).

30. Claudius and the Praetorians

1. Suet. *Div. Claud.* 10. 2 and 4. Latentem (sc. Claudium) discurrens forte gregarius miles, animadversis pedibus, studio sciscitandi quisnam esset, adgnovit extractumque prae metu ad genua sibi adcidentem imperatorem salutavit . . . In castra delatus est tristis ac trepidus

... Receptus intra vallum inter excubias militum pernoctavit, aliquanto minore spe quam fiducia ... Verum postero die ... armatos pro contione iurare in nomen suum passus est promisitque singulis quina dena sestertia, primus Caesarum fidem militis etiam praemio pigneratus (of AD 41).

2. Dio Cass. 60. 1. 2 f. κἄν τούτῳ στρατιῶταί τινες ἐς τὸ παλάτιον, ὅπως τι συλήσωσιν, ἐσελθόντες εὗρον τὸν Κλαύδιον ἐν γωνίᾳ που σκοτεινῇ κατακεκρυμμένον ... ἔπειτα δὲ γνωρίσαντες αὐτοκράτορά τε προσηγόρευ-σαν καὶ ἐς τὸ στρατόπεδον αὐτὸν ἤγαγον ... πᾶν τὸ κράτος αὐτῷ ἔδωκαν.

Suet. *Div. Claud.* 10. 2 and 4. A common soldier happened to run by, saw his feet, looked to see who it was, recognized Claudius in his hiding-place, and pulled him out. Claudius fell to his knees in fear, but the soldier hailed him as emperor ... He was borne off to the barracks, fearful and trembling ... Once inside the fortifications he passed the night among the sentries, with little confidence and less hope ... But the next day ... he had to allow an assembly of the soldiers to swear loyalty to him, and promised to pay 15,000 sesterces to each man—being the first of the Caesars to pledge monetary reward for military loyalty.

Dio Cass. 60. 1. 2 f. Meanwhile various soldiers had entered the palace, looking for loot, and found Claudius hidden in some dark corner ... Recognizing him, they saluted him as emperor, and led him off to their barracks ... They gave him supreme power.

30a   **30b**

a RIC I², p. 122, no. 7. Aureus of Rome, AD 41–2. *Obv.* TI(*berius*) CLAVD(*ius*) CAESAR AVG(*ustus*) P(*ontifex*) M(*aximus*) TR(*ibun-icia*) P(*otestate*), Head of Claudius, laureate. *Rev.* IMPER(*ator* or -*atore*) RECEPT(*us* or -*o*), above a battlemented wall enclosing the

Praetorian barracks, in which stands a figure holding a spear in front of an *aquila*, with a pedimented building behind.

b RIC I², p. 122, no. 12. Denarius of Rome, AD 41–2. *Obv.* As last coin. *Rev.* PRAETOR(*iani* or -*ianis*) RECEPT(*i* or -*is*), Claudius, bareheaded and wearing toga, standing clasping hands with soldier bearing shield and holding *aquila*.

See also *RIC* I², p. 122, no. 8 (denarius) and no. 11 (aureus).

After the assassination of Gaius the senate was permitted the brief luxury of discussing the future form of government at Rome (Dio Cass. 60. 1. 1), and, led by the consuls, it occupied the forum and the adjoining Capitol with the urban cohorts, being determined to claim *communis libertas*. But the still vague senatorial plans were thwarted by the swift action of a single Praetorian soldier on the look-out for palace valuables: instead, he found Claudius. On the following day Claudius had to pay an enormous price for the confidence which the Praetorians virtually forced him to accept. The sum of 15,000 sestertii per man which he now promised, and afterwards had to pay, can be expressed as 3,600 denarii or as 144 aurei per man; and if there were some 5,000 or more Praetorians to be rewarded at that rate, Claudius was thus faced with the provision of about 750,000 aurei or 19 million denarii.

Suetonius rightly emphasized this, the first occasion on which a *princeps* openly purchased military loyalty, as distinct from the discharge of a predecessor's legacy (see no. **27** above). He could, equally, have emphasized the size of the sum now involved—fifteen times as much as the legacies of Augustus and Tiberius. This is sufficient explanation of the two conspicuous 'praetorian' types of AD 41–2 (*a* and *b*) which were continued in 43–4 and 44–5 and (for at any rate one of the two types) in 46–7 (cf. *RIC* I², pp. 122f.): Dio Cass. (60. 12. 4) records that on every anniversary of his coming to power Claudius gave the Praetorians 100 sesterces (= 25 denarii) a man: his dependence upon them was plainly very real (cf. Tac. *Ann.* 11. 30, *matrimonium Silii vidit populus et senatus et miles*, and Campbell, *ERA*, pp. 109–20). The small figure in the *Imper Recept* type, with spear and *aquila*, has usually been identified as 'a soldier' (*BMCRE* I, p. 165, no. 5). However, C. L. Clay has recently proposed (*Num. Zeitschr.* 96, 1982, p. 43) that the figure is that of the female Fides Praetorianorum (cf. the *aliquanto minore spe quam fiducia* of Suetonius), an interpretation which would accord suitably with the expansion of the legend to IMPER(*ator* or -*atore*) RECEPT(*us* or -*o in fidem praetorianorum*). It would, similarly, underline the point of the *Praetor Recept* type. Mattingly (*BMCRE* I, p. cliii) explained this as 'praetorianus receptus' (i.e. in fidem), without specifically noting the fact that a handshake between emperor and soldier would be a normal gesture of mutually expressed *fides* (for the frequency of the clasped-hands motif cf. *RIC* I², p. 296). Clay has taken account of this, and, having preferred the ablative absolute in the resolution of IMPER RECEPT, he expands the companion legend similarly, as PRAETOR(*ianis*) RECEPT(*is in fidem imperatoris*). One could, of course, as easily read PRAETOR(*iani*) RECEPT(*i in fidem imperatoris*), with the nominative here (as it would with the other type as well) providing an accurately literal caption to explain the pictorial scene. Instinsky (in *Hamburger Beiträge zur Numismatik* 1953, p. 7) had earlier proposed *praetor*(io) *recept*(us).

31. Claudius' birth at Lugdunum

1. Suet. *Div. Claud.* 2. 1. Claudius natus est Iullo Antonio Fabio Africano conss. Kal. Aug. (1 August 10 BC) Lugduni eo ipso die quo primum ara ibi Augusto dedicata est, appellatusque Tiberius Claudius Drusus.

Suet. *Div. Claud.* 2. 1. Claudius was born at Lugdunum on 1 August during the consulships of Iullus Antonius and Fabius Africanus, on the very same day as that on which the altar there was dedicated to Augustus, and he was named Tiberius Claudius Drusus.

31a

a RIC I², p. 120, no. 1. Quadrans of Lugdunum, AD 41(?). *Obv.*
TI(*berius*) CLAVDIVS CAESAR AVG(*ustus*) P(*ontifex*) M(*aximus*)
TR(*ibunicia*) P(*otestate*) IMP(*erator*), Head of Claudius, laureate.
Rev. ROM(*ae*) ET AVG(*usto*), Altar of Lugdunum, decorated with
corona civica, laurels, and Victories.

The dedication on 1 August 10 BC, in Augustus' presence, of
the great altar of *Roma et Augustus* at Lugdunum was reflected
thereafter on the great series of *aes* coins, struck without doubt
at that city and perhaps also at secondary mints in Gaul (cf. J.-
B. Giard, *Rev. Num.* 1967, pp. 119ff.), which showed the altar,
with the legend ROM ET AVG, and continued in production
until the end of Augustus' reign (*RIC* I², pp. 57f.). A similar
but much scarcer (and thus presumably much shorter) series
appeared under Tiberius (*RIC* I², p. 95, nos. 31f.), and
Mattingly suggested (*BMCRE* I, p. cxxx) that this series ter-
minated with the revolt of Sacrovir (Tac. *Ann.* 3. 40f.) in AD 21.
Its rarity, however, suggests a much briefer span. No *aes* can be
assigned to Lugdunum under Gaius, though it was probably
there that his initial aurei and denarii were struck in direct succession to those of Tiberius (cf. *RIC* I², pp. 102ff. and no. **26**
above).

The familiar type of the Lugdunum altar, with ROM ET
AVG legend appeared again on a very small issue of *aes*
quadrantes for Claudius. Their altar type leaves no doubt that
they were struck at Lugdunum. Their exact date is, however,
less certain. TR P, without numbering, could properly be
AD 41–2: it could also indicate an unnumbered tenure of tribunician power in later years of the reign (cf. *RIC* I², pp. 127f.).
Nevertheless, the fact that Claudius' first year as *princeps* in
AD 41–2 coincided with the 50th anniversary of his birth at
Lugdunum makes it most likely that these quadrantes, with
their 'Lugdunum' type, refer to his birth there, and that these
were in fact a commemorative birthday series. Claudius boasts
of his birth in Gallia Comata in the Table of Lyons (see Smallwood, *Documents . . . Gaius–Nero*, no. 369, col. 2, lines 26–9),
and he used the circumstance in his wish to help protégés to
enter the senate (cf. M. T. Griffin in *CQ* 1982, pp. 404–18).

No other Claudian coinage, in *aes* or precious metal, can be
attributed to Lugdunum.

32. Claudius and the *aes* coinage of Gaius

1. Dio Cass. 60. 22. 3. ἐκείνους μὲν δὴ τούτοις ἐτίμησαν, τῇ δὲ δὴ τοῦ
Γαΐου μνήμῃ ἀχθόμενοι τὸ νόμισμα τὸ χαλκοῦν πᾶν, ὅσον τὴν εἰκόνα
αὐτοῦ ἐντετυπωμένην εἶχε, συγχωνευθῆναι ἔγνωσαν. καὶ ἐπράχθη μὲν
τοῦτο, οὐ μέντοι καὶ ἐς βελτίον τι ὁ χαλκὸς ἐχώρησεν, ἀλλ᾽ ἀνδριάντας ἀπ᾽
αὐτοῦ ἡ Μεσσαλῖνα τοῦ Μνηστῆρος τοῦ ὀρχηστοῦ ἐποιήσατο (of AD 43).

Dio Cass. 60. 22. 3. To these, then (i.e. members of Claudius' family),
the senators gave these honours. But they were angered by their
memory of Gaius, and decreed that all the bronze coinage struck
with his portrait should be melted down. And this was done, yet the
bronze fared no better, for Messalina had statues of the dancer
Mnester made out of it.

The statement that the senate could even contemplate, let
alone achieve, the melting down of *all* the portrait-bearing *aes*
coinage of Gaius, is beyond belief. It was easy enough for the
acta of Gaius to be rescinded (Suet. *Div. Claud.* 11. 3) and for his
damnatio memoriae to be effected (Dio Cass. 60. 4. 6), but the
total quantity of the portrait-bearing *aes* coins issued between
AD 37 and 41, and by now circulating in Rome and Italy alone,
was immense. And yet Dio Cassius seems to speak with the
authority of one who had firm knowledge of the senate's
decree. A parallel story is told of Licinius and the gold coinage
of Constantine (*Fragm. Hist. Graec.* 4. 198; cf. Dio Cass., ed.
Boissevain, 3. 748, fragm. 187).

There is no evidence of a *princeps* ever attempting the actual
recall of a predecessor's coinage. Indeed, the evidence is to the
contrary, the most significant being Vitellius' recorded
acquiescence in the continuing currency of the coins of Nero,
Galba, and Otho (Dio Cass. 64. 6. 1). A previous coinage was
withdrawn (or more probably sifted out over a period by the
mensarii, or at the *aerarium* itself) only when it had become
worn to virtual illegibility (cf. the action of Trajan in AD 107;
Dio Cass. 68. 15. 3, and *BMCRE* III, pp. lxxxvi ff.), or when
currency reform, in reducing the weight-standard (as under
Nero; see no. 38 below), left earlier coinage circulating at a too
obviously heavy standard. The comprehensive τὸ νόμισμα τὸ
χαλκοῦν πᾶν of Dio Cassius' statement about the action under
Claudius cannot possibly imply that *all* Gaius' portrait-bearing

aes coinage was called in and melted down in AD 43, even though Claudius' own *aes* was coined in some abundance from AD 41 (*RIC* I², pp. 127f.). The action of the senate under Claudius cannot have amounted to much more than the symbolic destruction of a token number of Gaius' *aes* coins—enough, perhaps, if Dio Cassius is accurate (and his story may reflect a current anti-imperial joke), for Messalina to convert the metal into bronze statues of Mnester: the contents of the *aerarium* could well have supplied enough coins for this. Action of a similar if probably more spasmodic kind is seen in the deliberate defacement, by hammering, of a few still surviving coins of the equally hated Domitian as part of the *damnatio memoriae* (Suet. *Dom.* 23. 1) which followed his assassination also.

33. Claudius and the port of Ostia

1. Suet. *Div. Claud.* 20. 3. Portum Ostiae extruxit circumducto dextra sinistraque brachio et ad introitum profundo iam solo mole obiecta; quam quo stabilius fundaret, navem ante demersit, qua magnus obeliscus ex Aegypto fuerat advectus, congestisque pilis superposuit altissimam turrem in exemplum Alexandrini Phari, ut ad nocturnos ignes cursum navigia dirigerent.

2. Dio Cass. 60. 11. 1–4. λιμοῦ τε ἰσχυροῦ γενομένου … ἐς παντὰ τὸν μετὰ ταῦτα αἰῶνα πρόνοιαν ἐποιήσατο … ἡ χώρα ἡ πρὸς ταῖς τοῦ Τιβέριδος ἐκβολαῖς … ἀνωφελές σφισι τὸ κράτος τῆς θαλάσσης ἐποίει· ἔξω τε γὰρ τῶν τῇ τε ὡραίᾳ ἐσκομισθέντων … οὐδὲν τὴν χειμερινὴν ἐσεφοίτα … τοῦτ' οὖν συνιδὼν λιμένα τε κατασκευάσαι ἐπεχείρησεν … καὶ νῆσον ἐν αὐτῇ πύργον τε ἐπ' ἐκείνῃ φρυκτωρίαν ἔχοντα κατεστήσατο (of AD 42).

3. *CIL* xiv. 85 = Dessau, *ILS* 207. Ti(*berius*) Claudius Drusi f(*ilius*) Caesar Aug(*ustus*) Germanicus pontif(*ex*) max(*imus*) trib(*unicia*) potest(*ate*) VI cos. design(*atus*) IIII imp(*erator*) XII p(*ater*) p(*atriae*) fossis ductis a Tiberi operis portus caussa emississque in mare urbem inundationis periculo liberavit. (AD 46–7, from Ostia).

Suet. *Div. Claud.* 20. 3. He (Claudius) built the port of Ostia, enclosing it on right and left by protective arms, and placing a deep jetty to protect the entrance. In order to strengthen the foundations of this jetty he first sank a ship which had transported a great obelisk from Egypt, and piled slabs of stone on it, and he placed on top of it all a very high tower, modelled on the Pharos of Alexandria, so that ships could plot their course by the fire burning on it at night.

Dio Cass. 60. 11. 1–4. There had been a severe famine . . . and Claudius took thought for the whole future . . . The area by the mouth of the Tiber . . . nullified their command of the sea. Cargoes could be brought in for storage in the summer . . . but no winter traffic was possible . . . This he saw, and he undertook the building of a harbour . . . setting up an island with a beacon-tower upon it.

CIL xiv. 85 = *ILS* 207 = Smallwood, *Documents . . . Gaius–Nero*, no. 312b. Tiberius Claudius Caesar Augustus Germanicus, son of Drusus, chief priest, holder of tribunician power for the sixth time, designated consul for the fourth time, saluted as imperator for the twelfth time, father of his country, on the completion of the canals leading from the Tiber to the sea, necessitated by the harbour-works, whereby he freed the city of Rome from the danger of flooding.

33a

a RIC I², p. 162, nos. 178–83; *BMCRE* I, pp. 221 ff., nos. 131 ff. Sestertii of Rome, *c.*AD 64. *Obv.* NERO CLAVD(*ius*) CAESAR AVG(*ustus*) GER(*manicus*) P(*ontifex*) M(*aximus*) TR(*ibunicia*) P(*otestate*) IMP(*erator*) P(*ater*) P(*atriae*), Head of Nero, laureate, sometimes wearing aegis. *Rev.* AVGVSTI POR(*tus*) OST(*iae*) S C, Bird's-eye view of the harbour of Ostia; to left, crescent-shaped pier with portico, figure at sacrifice, and building at end; to right, crescent-shaped row of slipways or berths; between these and the pier, column on round base, and on the column a standing figure with sceptre; below, Neptune, naked but for cloak, reclining and holding rudder and dolphin; within the harbour, a varying number of ships, most commonly seven.

Suetonius' account states unequivocally that the construction of the new harbour at Ostia (on which see Meiggs, *Ostia*²), undertaken both to facilitate the year-round reception in safety of corn-ships from overseas (cf. Rickman, *CSAR*, s.v. Ostia; also B. Levick in *AJ Phil.* 1978, pp. 87 f.) and also (as the inscription records) to reduce the danger of flooding in the low-lying areas of Rome, was the work of Claudius. Nor was it at all delayed. Dio Cassius dates the undertaking to AD 42, and the Ostia inscription commemorates completion some four years later. Claudius paid careful attention to the safety and regularity of the corn supply from abroad (Suet. *Div. Claud.* 18. 1). He was the first *princeps* to strike a *Ceres Augusta* coin-type (*RIC* I², p. 127, no. 94, issued in great quantity); and he arranged for the stationing of fire-fighters at the new Ostian port (Suet. *Div. Claud.* 25. 2), where the granaries were very extensive. And even after the new harbour was in operation, temporary shortage of corn in AD 51 brought about something like mob violence in Rome (Tac. *Ann.* 12. 43).

Although the completion of the new port of Ostia could prompt epigraphic commemoration in AD 46–7, it must be presumed that subsequent work and improvement were found necessary, for Nero, whose *aes* coinage may have begun *c.*AD 62 (*RIC* I², pp. 137 ff.), did not strike his celebrated POR OST sestertii until *c.*64. These coins, which rank among the most splendidly detailed architectural and topographical designs in the imperial series, suggest that some elements in the original Claudian harbour may indeed have been changed. In particular, Suetonius speaks of a very high Pharos-like tower at the harbour entrance, from which warning fire could be seen at night; but the harbour on Nero's sestertii shows, instead, a sceptred figure on a column, hardly compatible with a warning fire. And if ten years did in fact elapse between Claudius' death and the completion of Neronian work on the harbour, it is not in itself improbable that other details of the Claudian plan were altered or improved (cf. the ambitious plan of Nero in Suet. *Nero* 16. 1). This would seem to be more likely than an alternative suggestion (Griffin, *Nero*, p. 107) that Nero's 'Ostia' sestertii may 'simply celebrate his concern for the corn supply of Rome'. Claudius' building of the port had taken place only two decades earlier, as most adults would clearly have remembered: Nero's additions and improvements were a matter of his own separate and individual credit. The work of the two emperors had produced, in combination, *Portus Ostiae Augusti*—the 'imperial' port of Ostia. The name of 'Port Augustus' comprehended the work of both emperors.

34. The power of Pallas under Claudius

1. Tac. *Ann.* 13. 14. Et Nero . . . demovet Pallantem cura rerum quis a Claudio impositus velut arbitrium regni agebat; ferebaturque degrediente eo magna prosequentium multitudine non absurde dixisse, ire Pallantem ut eiuraret. Sane pepigerat Pallas ne cuius facti in praeteritum interrogaretur paresque rationes cum re publica haberet (of AD 55).

2. Plin. *Epist.* 7. 29. 1 f. Ridebis, deinde indignaberis, deinde ridebis, si legeris, quod nisi legeris, non potes credere. Est via Tiburtina intra primum lapidem (proxime adnotavi) monimentum Pallantis ita inscriptum: 'Huic senatus ob fidem pietatemque erga patronos ornamenta praetoria decrevit et sestertium centies quinquagies, cuius honore contentus fuit'. (Cf. also Plin. *Epist.* 8. 6.)

Tac. *Ann.* 13. 14. Nero . . . removed Pallas from the responsibilities which Claudius had placed on him. Pallas, you might say, had been acting as the power behind the throne. The story now went that, as Pallas was departing with a great retinue of hangers-on, Nero aptly remarked 'There he goes to swear himself out of office.' Pallas had in fact stipulated that nothing in his past conduct should be questioned, and that his state accounts should be taken as balanced.

Plin. *Epist.* 7. 29. 1 f. You'll laugh, and then fume, and then laugh again if you read that which you'll not believe unless you read it. Before you reach the first milestone along the Tiburtine road (it is quite near, as I have checked for myself) there is a monument to Pallas inscribed as follows: 'To this man the senate decreed praetorian decorations and fifteen million sesterces on account of his good faith and his sense of duty towards his patrons; and he was satisfied by being thus honoured.

The freedman Pallas was Claudius' financial secretary *a rationibus* (Suet. *Div. Claud.* 28), and exercised power in more than purely financial affairs (cf. Griffin, *Nero*, pp. 29 f., and S. I. Oost in *AJ Phil.* 1958, p. 113). Together with his colleague Narcissus, the secretary *ab epistulis*, he had amassed great wealth (cf. the *tantum . . . adquirere et rapere* of Suetonius, ibid.; on freedmen generally see Millar, *ERW*, pp. 69–83). The young Nero, upon his succession to Claudius, wished to get rid of this great court potentate, and Pallas accepted his enforced retirement with equanimity, being strong enough to dictate his own terms—that no questions should be asked of him about his period in office, and that his account-books should be considered to be balanced. His recent proposal of a penalty on women who got married to slaves (Tac. *Ann.* 12. 53) had been well rewarded by the senate, with *ornamenta praetoria* and 15 million sesterces (= $3\frac{1}{4}$ million denarii = 150,000 aurei). It is of course impossible to say by how much more he had enriched himself while in office under Claudius.

One curious monetary feature of Claudius' principate has for long attracted attention. Plated denarii (i.e. coins having a base core plated with silver) had attested the skill and the enterprising industry of forgers for many years previously (cf. *BMCRE* I, p. xliv; M. Crawford in *Num. Chron.* 1968, pp. 55 ff.), and the low weight and occasionally faulty fabric of such plated coins had often prompted the use of a probe to test them. Under Claudius the proportion of plated denarii increased very notably. It is scarcely possible to attribute them to deliberate government policy, for substandard denarii—and the denarius was a basic element in military pay—would have severely impaired imperial credit. But it may be wondered if Pallas' unethical view of affairs of state allowed him either to profit directly from the production of a proportion of plated denarii or at least to make it easier for such malpractice to occur. Contact between the *a rationibus* and the mint of Rome would not have involved any great difficulty.

35. The younger Agrippina's prominence in AD 54

1. Tac. *Ann.* 12. 42. Nondum tamen summa moliri Agrippina audebat ni praetoriarum cohortium cura exolverentur Lusius Geta et Rufrius Crispinus . . . Transfertur regimen cohortium ad Burrum

Afranium, ... gnarum tamen cuius sponte praeficeretur. Suum quoque fastigium Agrippina extollere altius (of AD 51).

2. Tac. *Ann.* 13. 2. Propalam tamen omnes in eam (sc. Agrippinam) honores cumulabantur, signumque more militiae petenti tribuno dedit (sc. Nero) 'Optimae Matris' (of AD 54).

3. Suet. *Nero* 9. Matri summam omnium rerum privatarum publicarumque permisit (sc. Nero). Primo etiam imperii die signum excubanti tribuno dedit 'Optimam Matrem'.

4. Dio Cass. 61. 3. 2. καὶ τὸ μὲν πρῶτον ἡ Ἀγριππῖνα πάντα αὐτῷ τὰ τῇ ἀρχῇ προσήκοντα διῴκει ... ταῖς τε πρεσβείαις ἐχρημάτιζε καὶ ἐπιστολὰς καὶ δήμοις καὶ ἄρχουσι καὶ βασιλεῦσιν ἐπέστελλεν (of AD 54).

Tac. *Ann.* 12. 42. But Agrippina did not yet dare to make her greatest coup until Lusius Geta and Rufrius Crispinus could be removed from the command of the Praetorian cohorts ... The command was transferred to Afranius Burrus ... who was however well aware of the source of the wish by which he was being promoted. Agrippina continued with her own aggrandizement as well.

Tac. *Ann.* 13. 2. Every outward honour was heaped on Agrippina, and when a tribune asked for the watchword, according to military custom, Nero gave it as 'The Best of Mothers'.

Suet. *Nero* 9. Nero allowed his mother full authority in all business, public as well as private. On his first day as emperor he even gave the watchword 'The Best of Mothers' to the tribune of the watch.

Dio Cass. 61. 3. 2. At first Agrippina conducted all imperial business ... negotiating with embassies, and corresponding with communities, foreign magistrates, and kings.

35a   **35b**

a RIC I², p. 150, nos. 1 f. Aureus and denarius of Rome, AD 54. *Obv.* AGRIPP(*ina*) AVG(*usta*) DIVI CLAVD(*ii uxor*) NERONIS

CAES(*aris*) MATER, Confronting busts of Nero, bareheaded, and Agrippina. *Rev.* NERONI CLAVD(*io*) DIVI F(ilio) CAES(*ari*) AVG(*usto*) GERM(*anico*) IMP(*eratori*) TR(*ibunicia*) P(*otestate*), Oak-wreath enclosing EX S(*enatus*) C(*onsulto*).

b *RIC* I², p. 150, nos. 6f. Aureus and denarius of Rome, AD 55. *Obv.* NERO CLAVD(*ius*) DIVI F(*ilius*) CAES(*ar*) AVG(*ustus*) GERM(*anicus*) IMP(*erator*) TR(*ibunicia*) P(*otestate*) COS, Jugate busts of Nero (in the forefront), bareheaded, and Agrippina. *Rev.* AGRIPP(*ina*) AVG(*usta*) DIVI CLAVD(*ii uxor*) NERONIS CAES(*aris*) MATER, Quadriga of elephants bearing figures of Divus Claudius and Divus Augustus, with EX S C above.

The distinguished Julian lineage of the younger Agrippina had marked her out as a figure of major consequence even during the principate of her brother Gaius (cf. Griffin, *Nero*, pp. 25 ff., and no. **29** above), who found it expedient to banish her to the island of Pontia. Recalled thence after the death of Gaius in 41, she set about the active increase of her influence at court and over Claudius (Tac. *Ann.* 12. 1 ff.), and by 48 her claims to succeed Messalina as Claudius' next wife had prevailed (though not without some public hostility towards her) and her young son Nero was betrothed to Claudius' daughter Octavia—a step which promoted him to the level of Claudius' son Britannicus (Tac. *Ann.* 12. 9). It would have been in order to make her obviously very ambitious behaviour more acceptable to a critical public opinion that she succeeded in replacing the joint Praetorian prefects, Geta and Crispinus, by a single prefect, Burrus—her own nominee, and therefore trustworthy—in AD 51.

This joint advancement in the prestige and prospects of Agrippina and Nero was clearly, and deliberately, reflected in the aurei and denarii struck at Rome between AD 50 and 54. These included coins with obverse portraits and obverse legends of both the mother and the son (something never previously seen in the imperial coinage, where, apart from commemorative issues, the obverse had always shown the *princeps* of the day). They included also types recording Nero's supernumerary election to all four of the priestly *collegia*, his designation as consul, and his elevation as *princeps iuventutis* (*RIC* I², pp. 125 f., nos. 75–83; cf. Tac. *Ann.* 12. 41). No coinage of Rome whatsoever referred to Britannicus, four years Nero's

junior, who seems (Tac. *Ann.* ibid.) to have been systematically
slighted. His sole appearance on imperial coinage, as distinct
from provincial or purely local issues (cf. Griffin, *Nero*, p. 29f.),
had been on that of Caesarea in Cappadocia in AD 46, on a coin
showing him with Messalina, his sister Octavia, and his half-
sister Antonia (*RIC* I², p. 132, no. 124). It should be noted that
the *aes* sestertii formerly assigned to Claudius' reign because of
their obverse portraits of Britannicus (*BMCRE* I, p. 196,
no. 226 with note) are now given with high probability to the
principate of Titus as commemorative coins in honour of his
close boyhood friend (*BMCRE* II, pp. lxxviii and 293, no. 306;
cf. Suet. *Div. Tit.* 2).

Nero's succession to the principate at the age of 17 (Suet.
Nero 8. 1) found Agrippina with no less expectation than
experience of power; and the gold and silver of the mint of
Rome in AD 54 clearly confirm the historical tradition of
Tacitus, Suetonius, and Dio Cassius, showing her in a seeming
parity of imperial power. Even if the precise degree of her
power was perhaps not agreed by the ancient historians (cf.
Griffin, *Nero*, pp. 37 ff.; see also B. Levick in *Studies in Latin
Literature and Roman History* iii, *Coll. Latomus* 180, ed. C. De-
roux (Brussels, 1982), pp. 222–5), the fact remains that she was
the first empress to share lifetime portraiture on coinage with a
reigning *princeps*. But her hunger for power (cf. the *ferocia Agrippinae* of Tac. *Ann.* 13. 2) was to be quickly checked by the
unpredictable alliance of Nero's mentor Seneca and her own
original protégé Burrus, the Praetorian prefect (see no. 36
below). In AD 54 the coin-portraits of Agrippina and Nero were
on an equal plane (see *a*), but in 55 the portrait of Nero had
primacy over that of Agrippina, whose titles now replaced those
of Nero on the reverse (see *b*, for the type of which cf. Tac. *Ann.*
12. 69). From 55–6 until her death in 59, when Nero publicly
attacked her past behaviour (Tac. *Ann.* 14. 11), the imperial
coinage made no further reference to her. The aurei and
denarii struck at Rome (*pace* J. van Heesch, *Rev. Belge* 1980,
pp. 249ff.) from 55–6 to 63–4 present a totally different
uniformity of types, which, considered in association with the
initial Neronian types of 54–5, lie at the very heart of the arguments concerning the direction and purpose of imperial coin-
types (see most recently Sutherland, *Rev. Num.* 1983, pp. 73ff.).

36. The influence of Seneca and Burrus from AD 54

1. Tac. *Ann.* 13. 2–5. Hi (sc. Seneca and Burrus) rectores imperatoriae iuventae . . . diversa arte ex aequo pollebant . . . Certamen utrique unum erat contra ferociam Agrippinae . . . Die funeris (sc. of Claudius) laudationem eius princeps exorsus est . . . Oratio a Seneca composita . . . Adnotabant seniores . . . primum ex iis qui rerum potiti essent Neronem alienae facundiae eguisse . . . Peractis tristitiae imitamentis curiam ingressus et de auctoritate patrum et consensu militum praefatus, consilia sibi et exempla capessendi egregie imperii memoravit . . . Tum formam futuri principatus praescripsit . . . discretam domum et rem publicam. Teneret antiqua munia senatus . . . Nec defuit fides (of AD 54).

2. Dio Cass. 61. 4. 1. αὐτοὶ (sc. Seneca and Burrus) τὴν ἀρχὴν ἅπασαν παρέλαβον, καὶ διῴκησαν ἐφ᾽ ὅσον ἠδυνήθησαν ἄριστα καὶ δικαιότατα, ὥσθ᾽ ὑπὸ πάντων ἀνθρώπων ὁμοίως ἐπαινεθῆναι . . . καὶ συμφρονήσαντες αὐτοὶ μὲν πολλὰ τὰ μὲν μετερρύθμισαν τῶν καθεστηκότων τὰ δὲ καὶ παντελῶς κατέλυσαν, ἄλλα τε καινὰ προσενομοθέτησαν (of AD 54).

Tac. *Ann.* 13. 2–5. Seneca and Burrus guided the emperor's youth . . . Their skills were different, but they had equal influence. They were united in a single struggle, against the fierce spirit of Agrippina . . . On the day of Claudius' funeral Nero pronounced the eulogy . . . the speech had been written by Seneca . . . The older men present . . . remarked that Nero was the first emperor to need another man's eloquence . . . With this show of sorrow ended, Nero entered the Senate House, talked of the authority of the senators and the unity of the army, and called to mind the counsels and the examples which he had in taking over the empire with distinction . . . He then laid down the pattern of his future government . . . 'The imperial house and the state shall be distinct. Let the senate keep its traditional powers.' He was as good as his word.

Dio. Cass. 61. 4. 1. Seneca and Burrus took over the entire government, and conducted it so far as they could in the best and most just manner, so that they gained universal praise. They thought alike, and in many respects changed previous methods: some things they did away with entirely, while in others they introduced new legislation.

36a   *36c*   *36d*

a *RIC* I², p. 151, nos. 8 f. Aureus and denarius of Rome, AD 55–6.
  Obv. NERO CAESAR AVG(*ustus*) IMP(*erator*), Nero's youthful
  head, bare. *Rev.* PONTIF(*ex*) MAX(*imus*) TR(*ibunicia*) P(*otestate*)
  II P(*ater*) P(*atriae*) around oak-wreath enclosing EX S(*enatus*)
  C(*onsulto*).

b *RIC* I², p. 151, nos. 21 f. Aureus and denarius of Rome, AD 60–1.
  Obv. As last coin, with Nero's features thickening. *Rev.* PONTIF
  MAX TR P VII COS IIII P P around oak-wreath enclosing EX
  S C.

c *RIC* I², p. 152, nos. 27 f. Aureus and denarius of Rome, AD 60–1.
  Obv. As last coin. *Rev.* Legend as last coin, with EX S C; Roma in
  military dress, with foot on helmet by dagger and bow, inscribing
  shield.

d *RIC* I², p. 153, nos. 44 f. Aureus and denarius of Rome, *c.*AD 64–
  5. *Obv.* NERO CAESAR AVGVSTVS, Head of Nero, laureate,
  with gross features. *Rev.* AVGVSTVS AVGVSTA, Nero, togate
  and with radiate crown, standing beside empress (Poppaea), veiled
  and draped: he holds sceptre, she patera and cornucopia.

Tacitus' acute analysis of the combined gifts of Seneca, the
philosopher senator, and Burrus, the *praefectus praetorio* since
AD 51 (Tac. *Ann.* 12. 42), does not fully explain the steps by
which these two very dissimilar men, *rarum in societate potentiae
concordes* (Tac. *Ann.* 13. 2), jointly contrived to divert the power
of Agrippina (see no. 35) and to bring such great initial influence to bear on the young Nero, still only in his seventeenth
year when he succeeded Claudius. Nor is the degree of Nero's
reliance on Seneca and Burrus in his early years of power at all

clear. 'Shall we believe with Dio that Nero left the decisions to others, or with Suetonius that he was in full control, or with Tacitus that he was active under guidance?' (Griffin, *Nero*, p. 40, and the same author's *Seneca*; also B. Levick in *Coll. Latomus*, 180 (1982), pp. 211–25 (see no. 35)). About two things, however, there can be little doubt. From the very first Seneca and Burrus, both of them *amici principis* (that is, personal and confidential advisers), set out to curb the formidable influence of Agrippina: Mattingly observed (*BMCRE* I, p. clxxi) that the governing circles of Rome had under Claudius become deeply 'hostile to feminine influence in serious politics'. And both Tacitus and Dio Cassius are explicit about the administrative changes effected by the two *amici principis*: *multa . . . arbitrio senatus constituta sunt* (Tac. *Ann.* 13. 5).

One reflection of administrative change is to be seen in the aurei and denarii coined at Rome from AD 55–6 (no *aes* was to be coined under Nero until *c.*AD 62; cf. *RIC* I², pp. 137 ff.). Every gold and silver coin of Rome from 55–6 down to 63–4 restricted its legends to the minimally correct recital of Nero's constitutional powers (see *a–c*), and also showed, from 55–6 down to 60–1, the uniformly constitutional type of the *corona civica*, which since Gaius' principate had signified constitutional accession (cf. *RIC* I², pp. 109, no. 19; 111, no. 37; 122, no. 5; 128, no. 96). More remarkable still, and beginning even when Agrippina's power had not yet been broken, was the fact that every coin of gold and silver struck at Rome from 54 to 63–4 (with the exception of one very rare issue of half-aurei) bore the formula EX S C.

The significance of the plain S C on *aes* coins from Augustus onwards (see no. 14 above) is probably to be understood (*pace* Griffin, *Nero*, pp. 58 f.) as denoting the agency of the senate in requisitioning and withdrawing supplies of *aes* from the *aerarium* for coinage. S C had never appeared on the gold and silver of the empire except for very rare cases (cf. *RIC* I², p. 64, no. 321) where, like S P Q R (cf. *RIC* I², pp. 68 f., nos. 360, 369), it denoted the source of an honour to the *princeps* shown by the actual type. This being so, it will of course be argued that the EX S C on Nero's earlier gold and silver should have a parallel meaning; and at first this argument appears to be plausible, seeing in the EX S C of Nero's coinage the senatorial vote of the *corona civica* to him. However, when the *corona civica* type was dropped in the course of AD 60–1, and was replaced by figure-types, the EX S C was continued (see *c*); and considerable effort is involved if we are to interpret these figure-types—two of which are Roma and Ceres—as honours paid to Nero by the senate (argued by C. L. Clay, *Num. Zeitschr.* 1982, pp. 33 ff., 50 f.). It seems altogether more likely to suppose that, while all emperors from Augustus onwards had exercised their *imperium* over stocks of gold and silver in the *aerarium*, Seneca and Burrus transferred this control (perhaps even away from the grasping hands of Agrippina?) back to the *arbitrium* of the senate, where it had lain until the time of Julius Caesar (see no. 1 above). Dio Cassius specifically recorded that 'they legally rearranged much previous practice', and the EX S C of Nero's gold and silver ('consequential upon a decree of the senate') seems to furnish a clear example of the new legislation which they prompted. Burrus, the military member of the partner-ship, would have had no doubt of the necessity of safeguarding those stocks of gold and silver which were the primary source of army pay: it should be noted that, even though no *aes* was struck until *c.*62, dated gold and silver were issued in every year down to 63–4.

From 64, however, the character of Nero's gold and silver coinage underwent a radical change. Not only was its standard of weight (and also fineness) reduced (see no. 38 below), but it ceased to bear an annual dating (see *d*) and its type-content, hitherto a correct statement of Nero's constitutional position, was designed to focus in a purely personal way upon him.

37. Nero as a public performer

1. Tac. *Ann.* 14. 14 f. Vetus illi (sc. Neroni) cupido erat curriculo quadrigarum insistere nec minus foedum studium cithara ludicrum in modum canere. Concertare equis regium et antiquis ducibus facti-tatum memorabat . . . Cantus Apollini sacros, talique ornatu adstare . . . Romana apud templa numen praecipuum et praescium . . . Instituit ludos Iuvenalium vocabulo . . . Ipse scaenam incedit, multa cura temptans citharam (of AD 59).

2. Tac. *Ann.* 15. 74. Reperio in commentariis senatus Cerialem Anicium consulem designatum pro sententia dixisse ut templum divo Neroni . . . publica pecunia poneretur (of AD 65).

3. Suet. *Nero* 25. 1 f. Reversus e Graecia . . . Palatium et Apollinem petit . . . Sacras coronas in cubiculis circum lectos posuit, item statuas suas citharoedico habitu, qua nota etiam nummum percussit.

4. Dio Cass. 62. 20. 1 and 21. 1. . . . παρῆλθέ τε καὶ αὐτὸς ὁ Νέρων ἐς τὸ θέατρον . . . καὶ ἔστη . . . ἐπὶ τῆς σκηνῆς ὁ Καῖσαρ τὴν κιθαρῳδικὴν σκευὴν ἐνδεδυκώς . . . ἀγῶνα πενταετηρικὸν κατεστήσατο, Νερώνεια αὐτὸν ὀνομάσας (of AD 59–60).

Tac. *Ann.* 14. 14 f. Nero had a long-standing desire to drive a four-horse chariot, and an equally unpleasant wish to sing to the lyre, in theatrical fashion. He would remind people that it was a royal custom to compete with horses, and that this had often been done by past leaders . . . Songs were sacred to Apollo, he said, and it was in the dress of a singer that this eminent and prophetic divinity was to be seen standing in Roman temples . . . He founded the games called Iuvenalia . . . He himself mounted the stage, tuning his lyre with great care.

Tac. *Ann.* 15. 74. I find in the senatorial records that Anicius Cerealis, a consul-designate, formally proposed the erection of a temple to the divine Nero at the public expense.

Suet. *Nero* 25. 1 f. On his return from Greece . . . Nero made for the Palatine and the temple of Apollo . . . In his bedchambers he placed his sacred crowns around the beds, as well as statues of himself dressed as a lyre-player: he even had this design struck as a type for a coin.

Dio Cass. 62. 20. 1 and 21. 1. Nero himself came into the theatre . . . the emperor took his stand . . . on the stage, dressed as a lyre-player . . . He established a five-yearly contest which he named the Neronia.

37a

37b

a *RIC* I², p. 158, nos. 73–82 (cf. p. 163, nos. 205–12). As of Rome, *c*.AD 62. *Obv.* NERO CLAVDIVS CAESAR AVG(*ustus*) GERMA(*nicus*), Head of Nero, bare, laureate, or radiate. *Rev.* PONTIF(*ex*) MAX(*imus*) TR(*ibunicia*) P(*otestate*) IMP(*erator*) P(*ater*) P(*atriae*), Apollo Citharoedus in flowing robes advancing and playing the lyre.

b *RIC* I², p. 159, nos. 103–8 (cf. p. 162, nos. 163–77). Sestertius of Rome, *c*.AD 63. *Obv.* NERO CLAVDIVS CAESAR AVG(*ustus*) GERM(*anicus*) P(*ontifex*) M(*aximus*) TR(*ibunicia*) P(*otestate*) IMP(*erator*) P(*ater*) P(*atriae*), Head of Nero, laureate, sometimes wearing aegis. *Rev.* DECVRSIO, Nero on prancing horse, with a foot-soldier holding vexillum preceding him, and another foot-soldier behind him.

c *RIC* I², pp. 164f., nos. 228–48. Semis of Rome, *c*.AD 64. *Obv.* NERO CAESAR AVG(*ustus*) IMP(*erator*), Head of Nero, bare or laureate. *Rev.* CERTA(*men*) QVINQ(*uennale*) ROM(*ae*) CO(*nstitutum*), S(*emis*), S C, Decorated table bearing urn and wreath.

Whether or not it is true, as Dio Cassius records (61. 4. 1), that the careful administrative regime instituted by Seneca and Burrus left Nero with too little work to do (ἔχαιρεν ἐν ῥᾳστώνῃ διάγων) from AD 54 (see no. **36** above), by AD 59 he had fully developed his passion for personal and public participation in artistic and other competitive festivals (cf. Griffin, *Nero*, pp. 41 ff., 109 ff., 160 ff.; E. Rawson in *PBSR* 1981, pp. 1–16, argues for the respectability of chariot-racing for the upper class). This passion resulted, incidentally, in the rare instance of an ancient author commenting on an imperial coin-type: Suetonius would have seen for himself, some fifty years later, coins of Nero's 'Apollo' type (see *a*) still in circulation, even if

rather worn by then, for they were produced in some abundance. Considerable and increasing adulation attended Nero's
person and his public performances from this time onwards, so
that by 65 flattery in the senate could go so far as to propose the
building of a temple to him as a living *divus*. Nero, indeed,
rejected this proposal; but from *c*.63 he had allowed his portrait
on the *aes* dupondii of Rome (as also of Lugdunum from *c*.64)
to be shown wearing the radiate crown of divinity (*RIC* I²,
pp. 159 f., 173 f.). This, previously accorded only to a *divus* after
death (cf. *RIC* I², pp. 98 f., 108 ff., 150), was henceforth to
become the normal (and curiously illogical) distinguishing
mark of the dupondius. Between *c*.63 and 65, moreover, Nero's
coin portraits quite often showed him wearing the aegis (*RIC*
I², pp. 159 ff.).

His *aes* coinage—the coinage of maximum circulation in
Rome itself—reflected his theatrical sense of prestige in other
ways too. The *decursio*, a military parade by the praetorians,
provided him with a prominent equestrian role, advertised on
conspicuously beautiful sestertii (see *b*), and the institution of
the *certamen quinquennale* in AD 60 was commemorated on *aes*
semisses with one form or another of a celebratory legend (*c*):
these little coins were struck in very large numbers, and must
be presumed to have played a suitable part in the attendance of
the *plebs urbana* at the *certamen*.

It should be observed that the *aes* of Rome struck *c*.AD 62–3
lacked the formula S C (see *a* and *b*). This formula had been
normal on all previous *aes* from Augustus onwards except the
Adlocut(io) *Coh*(ortium) sestertii of Gaius (see no. 27 above).
Various reasons may be suggested for its omission *c*.62–3. It is
possible that when the restraining counsels of Seneca and
Burrus upon him had slackened, Nero not only reclaimed the
old imperatorial rights over gold and silver coinage (see no. 36
above) but first, at least temporarily, extended his supreme
control over the *aes* in the *aerarium* (cf. *RIC* I², pp. 137 ff.). Or it
may be supposed, perhaps more probably, that the omission of
S C from Nero's *aes* coinage *c*.62–3 was the result of his
omission either to record the passing of a *senatus consultum*
authorizing the appropriation of metal for that coinage, or even
to trouble to have one passed at all. Relations between Nero
and the senate were certainly deteriorating by this time (cf.

Griffin, *Nero*, pp. 112 ff.). Whatever its cause, however, omission was only temporary. From *c*.64 onwards, Nero's *aes* once more bore the formula S C.

38. Nero's reduction of the weight of aurei and denarii

Pliny, *NH* 33. 3. Postea (i.e. for the period of Julius Caesar and the *triumviri rei publicae constituendae*) placuit ✷ (i.e. *denarios aureos*) XXXX signari ex auri libris, paulatimque principes imminuere pondus et novissime Nero ad XXXXV.

Pliny, *NH* 33. 3. Afterwards it was decided that 40 aurei should be struck from a pound of gold. Emperors gradually lightened the weight, until Nero most recently reduced the figure to 45.

After the collapse of the Republic proper, it would appear from Pliny that an official decision was taken (*placuit*) to reduce the weight of the aureus to $\frac{1}{40}$ of a Roman pound (for which see *BMCRE* I, pp. 1 ff.). His statement that emperors thereafter reduced this standard gradually, until Nero's clear-cut reduction took place, requires qualification. Aurei from Augustus to Claudius, and indeed to Nero's first decade of power, show that Augustus struck aurei at $\frac{1}{41}$ of a pound of gold; Tiberius, Gaius, and Claudius at $\frac{1}{42}$; and Nero, until AD 64, at $\frac{1}{43}$. These figures are derived from the weights of large numbers of surviving coins, with careful allowance made for wear. Silver denarii followed a similar downward course. Those of Augustus weighed $\frac{1}{84}$ of a pound of silver; those of Tiberius, Gaius, and Claudius $\frac{1}{85}$; and those of Nero, until AD 64, $\frac{1}{89}$ (*RIC* I², p. 134). Pliny therefore failed to record that from AD 14 to 54 the weight-standards of both aurei and denarii remained without change; and permanence of standards over a period of forty years strongly suggests the existence in the mint of Rome during that period of a set of official standard weights. Nor did Pliny explicitly record that from AD 54 to 64 (during most of which years Seneca and Burrus exerted their joint influence on administrative affairs) there was a falling-off in weight-standards, very slight for gold, less so for silver. He was, however, correct in his statement that the aureus dropped to $\frac{1}{45}$ of a pound of gold under Nero (from AD 64, as we now know), who also reduced the denarius to $\frac{1}{96}$ of a pound of silver. These reductions are plainly seen in the gold and silver from AD 64, when the weight-peak of aurei dropped from $c.7.70-7.60$ g to $c.7.40-7.25$, and that of denarii from $c.3.65-3.55$ to $c.3.50-3.20$ (RIC I², pp. 150, 152).

The reasons for weight reductions at any period can only be a matter of speculation. At times when standards were held steady, as from Tiberius to Claudius, the foregoing suggestion of adherence to a set of standard weights kept at the mint appears to be a likely one. But when the level of weight crept down only marginally, as under Augustus, Tiberius, and the earlier years of Nero, it may well be that former standard weights were destroyed and new ones made, based in each case on the least worn coins of the preceding period (cf. my EC, p. 129, based on S. Bolin, $State and Currency in the Roman Empire to AD 300$, though I would now see the process as being less systematic). The reasons for such marginal reductions in weight could, in fact, have been various. That which occurred under Nero in the years AD 54–64, for example, could have reflected the cautious reaction of the Seneca–Burrus regime to a tendency towards rising prices. Then again, in AD 56 a change was made in the control of the $aerarium$ (Tac. $Ann.$ 13. 28). In 58 Nero aroused general consternation by his proposal to abolish the $vectigalia$ (Tac. $Ann.$ 13. 51); in that same year vigorous war was resumed against Parthia (Tac. $Ann.$ 13. 34), to be followed fairly quickly by war in Britain (Tac. $Ann.$ 14. 29ff.). It may, however, be questioned whether the conduct of warfare caused much abnormal expense. The army had to be paid whether in peace or war, and the chief items of additional expenditure would have been due to extra work at the armament factories and to the needs of busier transport, whether by land or sea. (A contrary view is argued by R. MacMullen in $Latomus$ 1984, pp. 571 ff.)

However, Nero's major weight reduction in AD 64, when the type-content of his precious-metal coinage was radically changed (RIC I², p. 153) and the purity of the actual metals clearly reduced (id., p. 5), was certainly due to the great fire at

Rome in that year (Tac. *Ann.* 15. 38 ff.), which was followed by apparently ruthless efforts to raise money for relief and massive reconstruction (Tac. *Ann.* 15. 45; cf. Dio Cass. 63. 22. 2, and Smallwood, *Documents . . . Gaius–Nero*, no. 391. For a modernizing view of Nero's actions see E. Lo Cascio in *JRS* 1981, p. 84). In itself, the reduction of 64 was not very great—a mere 2% for the aureus and a perhaps more significant 7% for the far more abundant denarius. Nevertheless it was sufficient, for the reduced standards introduced in 64 continued in force for very many years afterwards. And when Diocletian, c.AD 294, replaced a coinage of what was by then of disgracefully impure silver by a new and pure *argenteus*, he did so at the revised Neronian weight of $\frac{1}{96}$ of a pound, as the coins themselves showed with their bold reverse inscription XCVI.

39. The closing of the temple of Janus by Nero

1. Tac. *Ann.* 16. 23. Tempus damnationi (i.e. of Barea Soranus) delectum, quo Tiridates accipiendo Armeniae regno adventabat (of AD 66; the arrival of Tiridates in Rome would have been described by Tacitus in the now lost narrative following *Ann.* 16. 35).

2. Suet. *Nero* 13. 1 f. Non immerito inter spectacula ab eo (sc. Nero) edita et Tiridatis in urbem introitum rettulerim ... Ob quae imperator consalutatus, laurea in Capitolium lata, Ianum geminum clausit, tamquam nullo residuo bello.

3. Dio Cass. 63. 1. 2. καὶ ὁ Τιριδάτης ἐς τὴν Ῥώμην ... ἀνήχθη, καὶ ἐγένετο ... πομπὴ διὰ πάσης τῆς ἀπὸ τοῦ Εὐφράτου γῆς ὥσπερ ἐν ἐπινικίοις (of AD 66).

Tac. *Ann.* 16. 23. The moment chosen for the condemnation of Barea Soranus was that when Tiridates was approaching Rome to receive the sovereignty of Armenia.

Suet. *Nero* 13. 1 f. There is good reason for me to describe the entry of Tiridates into Rome among Nero's public shows ... It resulted in his salutation as 'imperator', the due bearing of a laurel to the Capitol, and the closing of the temple of the two-headed Janus, on the theory that no war was anywhere in progress.

Dio Cass. 63. 1. 2. And Tiridates was escorted to Rome . . . and there was a procession through the whole world from the Euphrates, as if in celebration of a military victory.

39a

a *RIC* I², p. 166, no. 263. Sestertius of Rome, AD 64–5. *Obv.* NERO CAESAR AVG(*ustus*) IMP(*erator*) TR(*ibunicia*) POT(*estate*) XI P(*ater*) P(*atriae*), Bust of Nero, laureate and cuirassed. *Rev.* PACE P(*opuli*) R(*omani*) TERRA MARIQ(*ue*) PARTA IANVM CLVSIT, S C, Partial view of the front of the temple of Janus, with latticed window and with garland hung across closed double doors.

Tacitus describes at length (*Ann.* 15. 29) Tiridates' symbolic act of homage, as king of Armenia, to Rome in Corbulo's presence in the east; and the narrative now lost from the end of *Ann.* 16 would doubtless have recounted the drama and excitement of his subsequent visit to Rome (for the celebrations there see M. P. Charlesworth in *JRS* 1950, pp. 69 ff.; for Nero's achievement in Armenia see Magie, *RRAM*, pp. 553–65, and K.-H. Ziegler, *BRP*, pp. 67–78). Suetonius records in some detail the magnificence of the ceremonies at Rome, and he implies quite clearly (*ob quae*) that these culminated in the formal closing of the temple of Janus—something not mentioned by Dio Cassius. The closing of this temple upon the extinction of all warfare in the Roman dominions (see no. 6 above) was always celebrated with the formula *pace terra marique parta* after a *senatus consultum* (cf. Gagé, *RGDA*, pp. 95 f.), and was now effected to mark the end of hostilities with Parthia.

Suetonius obviously regarded the ceremony as taking place in AD 66, on the occasion of Tiridates' visit to Rome. However, sestertii of the mint of Rome (*a*), unusual among Nero's *aes* coins in that they bear a tribunician dating (TR POT XI = AD 64–5) but not of any special rarity, indicate by their Janus temple type that the temple was closed not only before 66 but possibly as early as 64, as a consequence of Tiridates' symbolic act of homage in 63. The discrepancy has prompted modern comment (Griffin, *Nero*, p. 122). It has been noted that the arrangements for Tiridates' coronation in Rome were made in 63, when Nero in fact needed all the favourable publicity he could obtain (see Z. Yavetz in Levick (ed.), *AHM*, pp. 191 f.). As a result, the temple could have been ceremonially closed in 64. What does not seem possible is that Nero's Janus temple coins were 'issued in advance of the actual ceremony'. No numismatic parallel can be adduced for such an exception to the strictly annalistic character of the Roman coinage: no true parallelism can be easily found between Gaius' conceivable intention of issuing consecration coins in immediate honour of the dead Tiberius (see above, no. **26**) and the preparation of coins more than a year ahead of the closing of the temple. Equally it is difficult to accept (cf. Griffin, *Nero*, p. 267, note 12) the late statement by Orosius that Tacitus' *Histories* recorded the Janus temple as being open continuously from late in Augustus' reign to that of Vespasian, unless (in view of the silence of Tacitus in the *Annals* for AD 64) we are to suppose that Tacitus thought the closure of the temple to have occurred in 66 or later (i.e. after the extant part of *Ann.* 16), or intended to add the detail to an unfinished earlier narrative, or wished simply to imply that no closure took place—in clear contradiction to Suetonius' later record.

In connection with Suetonius' account of Nero's closure of the temple one should observe that Nero's sestertii show him, most unusually, both laureate and cuirassed: the *imperator* and his *laurea* are both emphasized. The Janus temple type was to be remarkably prominent on Nero's *aes* down to AD 67 (cf. *RIC* I², pp. 166–72), and a smaller version appeared on undated aurei and denarii of *c.*AD 64–6 (*RIC* I², p. 153). Tiridates' acceptance of Nero's suzerainty over Armenia, and the cessation of war with Parthia, were events of great moment, measured both by the publicity accorded to them and also by the cost to Rome of bringing Tiridates thither—over 500 million denarii for the actual journey, and another 50 million for his time in Rome, if Dio Cassius (63. 2. 2; 63. 6. 5) reported accurately.

40. Bullion-shortage after the fire of Rome in AD 64

1. Tac. *Ann.* 15. 45. Interea conferendis pecuniis pervastata Italia, provinciae eversae sociique populi et quae civitatium liberae vocantur. Inque eam praedam etiam dii cessere, spoliatis in urbe templis egestoque auro quod triumphis, quod votis omnis populi Romani aetas . . . sacraverat (of AD 64).

2. Tac. *Ann.* 16. 1. Inlusit dehinc Neroni fortuna per vanitatem ipsius et promissa Caeselli Bassi qui . . . mente turbida . . . vectus . . . Romam principis aditum emercatus expromit repertum in agro suo specum altitudine immensa, quo magna vis auri contineretur, non in formam pecuniae sed rudi et antiquo pondere (of AD 65).

3. Suet. *Nero* 31. 4. Ad hunc impendiorum furorem, super fiduciam imperii, etiam spe quadam repentina immensarum et reconditarum opum impulsus est ex indicio equitis R. pro comperto pollicitentis thesauros antiquissimae gazae . . . esse in Africa vastissimis specubus abditos.

4. Dio Cass. 62. 18. 5. χρήματα δὲ ὁ Νέρων παμπληθῆ καὶ παρὰ τῶν ἰδιωτῶν καὶ παρὰ τῶν δήμων . . . ἠργυρολόγησεν (of AD 64).

Tac. *Ann.* 15. 45. Meanwhile, in the effort to raise money, Italy was ravaged and provinces were ruined, together with allied and so-called 'free' communities. Even the gods yielded to this process of plunder: their temples in Rome were despoiled, and gold which Roman triumphs and Roman vows had universally hallowed through long ages was carried off.

Tac. *Ann.* 16. 1. Thereafter chance played a trick on Nero's credulity through the promises of a crazy fellow called Caesellius Bassus . . . Bassus sailed to Rome (i.e. from Africa), and, after buying his way into the emperor's presence, he explained that he had found on his land a cave of vast height which contained a great wealth of gold, not in the form of coin, but in the rough and heavy masses of olden days.

Suet. *Nero* 31. 4. Nero was encouraged in this hectic expenditure not only by the urgency of national credit but also by the sudden hope of vast hidden wealth reported to him by a Roman knight who gave him the certain promise that a hoard of very ancient treasure lay hidden in huge caves in Africa.

Dio Cass. 62. 18. 5. Nero collected money in huge amounts, both from individuals and from communities.

40b   *40c*

Types of Nero's aurei and denarii struck at Rome in

a AD 64–5.
AVGVSTVS AVGVSTA, gold and silver.
AVGVSTVS GERMANICVS, gold and silver.
CONCORDIA AVGVSTA, gold and silver.
IANVM CLVSIT PACE P R TERRA MARIQ PARTA, gold and silver.
IVPPITER CVSTOS, gold and silver.
ROMA, gold and silver.

b AD 65–6.
AVGVSTVS AVGVSTA, gold and silver.
IANVM CLVSIT etc., gold.
SALVS, gold and silver.
VESTA, gold and silver.

c AD 66–7.
IVPPITER CVSTOS, gold and silver.
ROMA, silver.
SALVS, gold and silver.

d AD 67–8.
Aquila (no legend), silver.
IVPPITER CVSTOS, silver.
ROMA, silver.
SALVS, silver.

For the chronology of these types, and commentary upon them, see
RIC I², pp. 145 ff.

The great fire of Rome, which took place at the height of the
summer in AD 64, left only four of the city's fourteen *regiones*
intact. The rest were either completely destroyed or very
seriously damaged (Tac. *Ann.* 15. 38–41). Work on rescue and
relief, and on subsequent rebuilding, was immense and urgent
(Tac. *Ann.* 15. 39 and 43), and involved high costs for demoli-
tion, clearance, transport of new building materials, and the
labour of rebuilding—all this, moreover, at a time when Nero's
extravagance was reaching new peaks (cf. no. 39 on the cost of
Tiridates' visit to Rome, and Tac. *Ann.* 15. 42 on the building of
Nero's new palace and the abortive Avernus–Tiber canal: for
his extravagance in general, Griffin, *Nero*, pp. 128 ff., 203 ff.).
Any reserves in the *aerarium* must soon have been used up, for
Tacitus and Dio Cassius agree on the immediacy of the efforts
made by Nero in 64 to raise money in Italy and elsewhere. That
the proceeds of those efforts were inadequate is suggested by
the story of Tacitus (for the year 65) and of Suetonius about the
'treasure of Dido' reported from North Africa. Suetonius even
records (*Nero* 32. 1) that the deception of Nero's hopes for this
treasure led to difficulty in paying the *stipendia* of the army,
though it is hard to believe that the army would have tolerated
postponement: perhaps this story was a generalization based
on one or two well-known incidents (cf. Campbell, *ERA*,
p. 173).

   It is reasonable to seek some reflection of these events in the
gold and silver coinage of Rome at the time. Dated aurei and
denarii ceased to be issued in AD 64, when the reduction of
weight-standards took place (see no. 38 above). The subsequent chronology of the precious-metal coinage is dependent
on a variety of factors—Nero's titulature (with the *praenomen
imperatoris* introduced in 66; cf. Griffin, *Nero*, pp. 232 f. with
notes 69 and 72), Nero's portraiture (with features advancing
from the gross to the very gross), and the probable historical
context of the reverse types employed (cf. *RIC* I², pp. 144 ff.). It
depends also upon the acceptance of the proposition that the
imperial coinage was produced on a system, first postulated by
Mattingly for a later period (*Num. Chron.* 1939, pp. 1 ff.) and

since then projected backwards in time (*RIC* I², pp. 15 f.), by which a given coin-type was allocated to an individual working-section, or *officina*, of the mint. Three *officinae* can certainly be seen at work under the three *tresviri monetales* of Augustus (see no. 13 above), as also at the Augustan mints of Ephesus and Pergamum (Sutherland, *The Cistophori of Augustus*), and a number of *officinae* varying from six to two can be made out with very fair probability for Claudius (*RIC* I², pp. 116 f.).

Under Nero there had from AD 60–1 to 62–3 almost certainly been three *officinae* at work for the three reverse types then being employed for the gold and silver (no *aes* was struck for Nero before *c*.62). In 64–5, however, six reverse types should show the operation of six *officinae*, implying a maximum output of aurei and denarii. But by *c*.65–6 the number of *officinae* had probably fallen to four, and *c*.66–8 even lower, to three. It must of course be borne in mind that the mint of Rome was producing a copious flood of *aes* between *c*.62 and 68 (*RIC* I², pp. 158–73), and that the range of *officinae* had to handle this as well as the aurei and denarii. Even so, the output of gold and silver certainly seems to have been contracted from *c*.65 onwards. Moreover, not only are the aurei and denarii of *c*.66–8 noticeably rarer than before, but aurei, which show a diminution *c*.66, do not seem to have been produced at all in 67–8. It would thus appear that Nero's heavy and indeed extravagant expenditure from 64 onwards caused a noticeable shortage of gold and silver bullion. If Nero had not committed suicide in June 68 that shortage would have become catastrophic, for the Iberian peninsula—then Rome's richest source of gold and silver by far—was united against him by its two military governors, Galba and Otho (cf. Sutherland, *NACQT* 1985, pp. 239 ff.).

41. Nero and the revolt of Vindex

1. Suet. *Nero* 40. 4. Neapoli de motu Galliarum cognovit . . . adeoque lente ac secure tulit ut gaudentis etiam suspicionem praeberet tamquam occasione nata spoliandarum iure belli opulentissimarum provinciarum.

2. Suet. *Nero* 41. 1. Edictis tandem Vindicis contumeliosis et frequentibus permotus senatum epistula in ultionem sui reique publicae adhortatus est.

3. Suet. *Nero* 42. 1. Postquam deinde etiam Galbam et Hispanias descivisse cognovit, conlapsus animoque male facto diu sine voce et prope intermortuus iacuit.

4. Dio Cass. 63. 22. 6. ἀνάστητε οὖν ἤδη ποτέ, καὶ ἐπικουρήσατε μὲν ὑμῖν αὐτοῖς, ἐπικουρήσατε δὲ τοῖς Ῥωμαίοις, ἐλευθερώσατε δὲ πᾶσαν τὴν οἰκουμένην (Vindex to his army, AD 68).

Suet. *Nero* 40. 4. It was at Naples that Nero learned of the Gallic revolt . . . and he took the news with such relaxed confidence that he led people to suspect that he rejoiced at the opportunity of despoiling very rich provinces by the justification of war.

Suet. *Nero* 41. 1. Stirred finally by the series of scornful edicts from Vindex, Nero wrote to the senate urging vengeance on his own behalf and that of the state.

Suet. *Nero* 42. 1. Learning afterwards that Galba and the Spanish provinces had also risen in revolt, Nero broke down and lay like one half dead, crazed and speechless.

Dio Cass. 63. 22. 6. Arise, therefore, rally to help yourselves, rally to help the Romans, set the whole world free.

41(1)   *41(2)*

Conspicuous legends on the coinage issued by Vindex in AD 68; see *RIC* I², pp. 206 ff.

GENIVS P(*opuli*) R(*omani*) / I(*uppiter*) O(*ptimus*) MAX(*imus*) CAPI-
TOLINVS
GENIVS P R / MARS VLTOR
GENIVS P R / SIGNA P R
HERCVLES ADSERTOR / FLORENTE FORTVNA P R

MARS VLTOR / SIGNA P R
MARS VLTOR / S P Q R
PAX ET LIBERTAS / SIGNA P R (1)
ROMA RESTITVTA / IVPPITER LIBERATOR
ROMA RESTITVTA / SIGNA P R
SALVS ET LIBERTAS / SIGNA P R (2)
SALVS GENE(*ris*) HVMANI / MARS VLTOR
SALVS GENERIS HVMANI / SIGNA P R
SALVS GENERIS HVMANI / S P Q R
VIRTVS / S P Q R

Suetonius devoted some five and a half chapters to the effect upon Nero, in and after March AD 68, of the news of the revolt of Vindex (with his proclaimed army of 100,000 men; Plut. *Galba* 4. 3) in Gaul, and of Galba's subsequent adherence to Vindex. Although Nero's thoughts were actively concerned with the mechanics and the operation of his new water-organ (Suet. *Nero* 41. 2), he was at the same time deeply disturbed by the 'repeatedly scornful' *edicta* which emanated from Vindex. These *edicta* could be held to include the *litterae* sent by Vindex to Galba (and duly and effectively publicized) urging him to stand forth as the *humano generi assertor* (Suet. *Galba* 9. 2; cf. Sutherland in *Num. Chron.* 1984, pp. 29 ff.). But they could also have been held to include (and would quite certainly have reflected) the extraordinarily defiant and outspoken series of denarii issued for Vindex in Gaul, possibly at Vienna (Vienne): Lugdunum, with its urban cohort, had refused to side with Vindex (Tac. *Hist.* 1. 65).

No such war of words had been waged in the Roman world since that between Octavian and Antony in the period before the battle of Actium (cf. K. Scott, *Mem. American Acad. Rome* 1933, pp. 1 ff.). Now, in AD 68, the barbed slogans on the coins of Vindex made it plain that the Gallic revolt was very far from being a mere outbreak of nationalism. They insisted on a Rome restored to the *Genius* of its people, on political liberation, freedom, and military vengeance, and on the primacy of the senate and people. There were, of course, purely local reasons which inflamed Gallic discontent, such as rapacious procurators and inordinate taxation (cf. Plut. *Galba* 4. 1; Dio Cass. 63. 22. 2). Primarily, however, the manifesto presented by the coinage of Vindex declares its origin in a morally outraged political consciousness. Nero's response, as recorded, was shocked and confused. There was a self-dramatizing pity for the first *princeps* to face the loss of power in his own lifetime. There was a phase of wild fury. There was a brave and glorious plan to lead an army into rebellious Gaul. Ultimately, there was inability to devise any positive resistance; and even though Vindex was defeated and killed by the army of Verginius Rufus, the initiative had then passed to Galba. (The events leading up to the fall of Nero are discussed by P. A. Brunt in *Latomus* 1959, pp. 531–59; and Griffin, *Nero*, pp. 185–234.)

All that Nero did was to exact, in advance, the compulsory year's rents to the imperial *fiscus*, insisting on payment in unworn and full-weight aurei and denarii (Suet. *Nero* 44. 2): this demand could have been a means of forcing those who had hoarded the heavier and finer pre-reform coins, selected for their unworn condition, to hand them over. He was trying, far too late, to supplement his stocks of gold and silver coin so seriously depleted since AD 64 (see no. 40 above).

42. The revolt of L. Clodius Macer against Nero

1. Tac. *Hist.* 1. 73. Per idem tempus expostulata ad supplicium Calvia Crispinilla ... periculo exempta est ... Transgressa in Africam ad instigandum in arma Clodium Macrum, famem populo Romano haud obscure molita, totius postea civitatis gratiam obtinuit (of Jan.–Mar., AD 69).

2. Suet. *Galba* 11. Nec prius usum togae reciperavit (sc. Galba) quam oppressis qui novas res moliebantur, praefecto praetori Nymphidio Sabino Romae, in Germania Fonteio Capitone, in Africa Clodio Macro legatis.

3. Plut. *Galba* 13. 3. ἔγραφε (sc. Nymphidius Sabinus) τῷ Γάλβᾳ δεδιττόμενος, νῦν μὲν, ὡς ὕπουλα καὶ μετέωρα πολλὰ τῆς πόλεως ἐχούσης, νῦν δὲ, Κλώδιον Μάκρον ἐν Λιβύῃ τὰ σιτηγὰ κατέχειν.

Tac. *Hist.* 1. 73. At the same period Calvia Crispinilla escaped danger, after her punishment had been demanded ... She had crossed over into Africa to urge Clodius Macer to take up arms, obviously attempting to bring about food-shortage for the people of Rome. Afterwards she earned the thanks of the whole state.

Suet. *Galba* 11. Galba did not resume the toga until the revolutionaries had been put down—the praetorian prefect Nymphidius Sabinus at Rome, and the two provincial governors, Fonteius Capito in Germany and Clodius Macer in Africa.

Plut. *Galba* 13. 3. Nymphidius Sabinus took to writing alarming letters to Galba, saying now that there was much hidden distemper and unrest at Rome, and now that Clodius Macer in Libya was holding back the corn-supplies.

42a   *42e*

a *RIC* I², p. 194, no. 6. Denarius of Carthage, *c.*Apr.–Oct. AD 68. *Obv.* L(*ucii*) CLODI MACRI LIBERATRIX, S C, Head of Africa in elephant-skin head-dress. *Rev.* LEG(*io*) I MACRIANA LIB(*eratrix*), Aquila between vexilla.

b *RIC* I², p. 194, no. 17. Denarius of Carthage, *c.*Apr.–Oct. AD 68. *Obv.* L CLODI MACRI, S C, Bust of Victory. *Rev.* LEG(*io*) III LIB(*eratrix*) AVG(*usta*), Aquila between vexilla.

c *RIC* I², p. 195, no. 29. Denarius of Carthage, *c.*Apr.–Oct. AD 68. *Obv.* L CLODI MACRI CARTHAGO, S C, Turreted bust of Carthago. *Rev.* ƧICILIA (*sic*), Medusa head on triskelis, its legs enclosing ears of corn.

d *RIC* I², p. 195, no. 30. Denarius of Carthage, *c.*Apr.–Oct. AD 68. *Obv.* ROMA, S C, Helmeted head of Roma. *Rev.* L CLODI MACRI, Trophy with two pointed shields.

e *RIC* I², p. 196, no. 41. Denarius of Carthage, *c.*Apr.–Oct. AD 68. *Obv.* L CLODIVS MACER, S C, Bare head of Clodius Macer. *Rev.* PRO PRAE(*tore*) AFRICAE, Warship with crew of oarsmen.

In comparison with their treatment of the rebellious movements of Vindex in Gaul and of Galba in Spain, the ancient historians paid only slight attention to the revolt in Africa of L. Clodius Macer, its *legatus Augusti propraetore*. Perhaps this was because it achieved nothing positive. Nevertheless, Macer may have looked dangerous at first. His power-base was in Numidia, where Legio III Augusta was stationed: he was able to take control of Carthage, which possessed a formidable harbour and naval dockyard (*Antiq. Journ.* 1979, pp. 19 ff.); and he was able to find money with which to raise another legion, I Macriana, to support his rising against Nero. The new legion and the previously existing III Augusta were now both formally styled *Liberatrix*.

It was almost certainly at Carthage that Macer set up a mint for the production of his now extremely rare denarii (no gold is known) for the payment of his legions and his civilian staff (cf. K. V. Hewitt, *Num. Chron.* 1983, pp. 64 ff.): the legend CARTHAGO and her bust (*c*) seem to be visible proof of this. All of Macer's denarii are conspicuous in that they bear the formula S C. This cannot be any sort of parallel to the EX S C on Nero's earlier gold and silver, which have been held to imply (see no. 36 above) direct senatorial access to gold and silver bullion in the *aerarium*. The S C of Macer's coins indicated that he, like Galba initially (cf. Suet. *Galba* 10. 1; Dio Cass. 63. 29. 6) professed his activity—and his coinage—to be on behalf of the senate against Nero. He certainly avoided any such title as *imperator*, and one series of his denarii bore a figure of Libertas (*RIC* I², p. 195, nos. 19–21)—appropriate on coins designed for payment to legions both styled *Liberatrix*. Others of his denarii suggest more clearly the ambitious direction of his thoughts. The *Sicilia* type with its corn-ears (*c*); the Roma type with its trophy (*d*); and the probably latest coins (*e*) with Macer's portrait, proprietary nominative legend, and warship—these indicate that, with or without encouragement from Calvia Crispinilla, his publicly professed object was to secure naval control of the central Mediterranean across to Sicily and thence to Rome, and thus also of the corn-ships sailing to Rome from Africa and Egypt (see Rickman, *CSAR*, pp. 67 ff., 231 ff.). Nymphidius Sabinus might well have hoped to make Galba nervous. But none of this happened. Galba, himself a recent

rebel in Spain, was now accepted by the senate: he could easily
regard Macer as *haud dubie turbantem*; and he had him put to
death some time in the early autumn of AD 68 (Tac. *Hist.* 1. 7).

43. *Adsertor* and *Salus* as concepts
for Vindex and Galba

1. Suet. *Galba* 9. 2. Carthagine nova conventum agens tumultuari
Gallias comperit (sc. Galba) legato Aquitaniae auxilia implorante;
supervenerunt et Vindicis litterae hortantis ut humano generi
assertorem ducemque se accommodaret.

2. Suet. *Galba* 10. 1 and 3. Igitur cum quasi manumissioni vacaturus
conscendisset (sc. Galba) tribunal . . . deploravit temporum statum
consalutatusque imperator legatum se senatus ac populi R. professus
est . . . Etiam per provincias edicta dimisit, auctor in singulis
universisque conspirandi simul et ut qua posset quisque opera
communem causam iuvarent.

Suet. *Galba* 9. 2. Galba was on circuit at New Carthage when he
learned that the Gallic provinces were in a ferment, with appeals for
help from the governor of Aquitania. And after that Vindex wrote to
Galba urging him to stand up for the freedom of the human race and
to undertake the leadership.

Suet. *Galba* 10. 1 and 3. Galba therefore ascended onto the platform
as if to apply himself to a manumission . . . and there he deplored the
state of the times. He was then hailed as *imperator*, but announced
formally that he was the delegate of the senate and people of Rome
. . . He also sent edicts through the provinces counselling a revolu-
tionary policy for all and sundry, so that everyone might in one way
or another help the common cause.

43a   *43c*

a *RIC* I², p. 204, no. 15. Denarius of Spain, *c.*Apr.–June, AD 68. *Obv.*
CONCORDIA HISPANIARVM ET GALLIARVM, Victory
standing facing on globe between confronting busts of Hispania
(on left, above cornucopia) and Gallia (on right, above oblong
shield). *Rev.* VICTORIA P(*opuli*) R(*omani*), Victory in biga.

b *RIC* I², p. 205, no. 28. Denarius of Spain, *c.*Apr.–June, AD 68. *Obv.*
LIBERTATI, Togate citizen, wearing cap of liberty, advancing
with wreath. *Rev.* S P Q R, Victory standing on globe and holding
wreath and palm.

c *RIC* I², p. 209, no. 70. Denarius of Gaul, *c.*Apr.–May, AD 68. *Obv.*
SALVS GENERIS HVMANI, Victory on globe holding wreath
and palm. *Rev.* SIGNA P(*opuli*) R(*omani*), Aquila between two
standards; altar to r. of aquila.

When C. Julius Vindex, *legatus pro praetore* of Gallia Lugdunensis, wrote early in AD 68 to Galba, now for eight years *legatus
proconsule* of Hispania Tarraconensis (Suet. *Galba* 8 f.), he urged
him to act as *assertor* of the human race and as *dux* (military
leader without formal grant of *imperium*) of a movement against
Nero. *Adsertor* was in fact very near in meaning to the word
vindex, one who championed the freedom of others (cf. no. **2**
above, and Donatus on Terence, *Adelphi* 2. 1. 40, *assertores
dicuntur vindices alienae libertatis*). Galba's response was cautious.
Aware already of Nero's suspicious hostility towards him (Suet.
Galba 9. 2), he began by deploring the turmoil of the times, and
even after his Spanish legion had formally saluted him as
imperator (a title always present on his later Spanish coinage; cf.
RIC I², pp. 232 ff.), he would assume no other public position
than that of *legatus* of the senate and people of Rome (i.e. not
any longer of Nero). The *edicta* which he then sent to the
provinces (primarily, it may be supposed, those of Spain and
Gaul), and in which he solicited combined help against Nero's
government, would have carried a considerable official weight.
Of the western provinces' individual responses we know that,
apart from Vindex, the instigator in Gallia Lugdunensis, Galba
won the support of Otho, governor of Lusitania (Suet. *Otho* 4.
1; Tac. *Hist.* 1. 13), and of Caecina, the quaestorian governor of
Baetica (Tac. *Hist.* 1. 53).

At this juncture the necessity began for Galba (cf. no. **44**
below) and for Vindex (cf. no. **41** above) to produce coinage

with which to pay their forces. This necessity is reflected in the
very numerous Spanish denarii on which neither Galba's name
nor his new status as *imperator* are to be seen, and in the equally
numerous and similarly anonymous Gaulish denarii prompted
by Vindex (cf. *RIC* I², pp. 203ff.). The Spanish denarii made
no reference to the concept of *adsertor*: they went no further
than to emphasize *Bonus Eventus*, *Genius Populi Romani*, *Mars
Ultor* (cf. no. 2 above), the common effort of the provinces of
Spain and Gaul, and *Libertas* (see *a* and *b*). Those produced in
Gaul for Vindex were more outspoken, and even featured
Hercules Adsertor (*RIC* I², p. 207, no. 49), their chief themes,
however, being *Salus Generis Humani* (*c*; an echo of Vindex's
original letter to Galba, who was himself now content with a
Salus Publica type; cf. *RIC* I², p. 206, no. 36) and *Signa P*(opuli)
R(omani) (*c*), with a type made famous 100 years earlier by the
still circulating pre-Actian denarii of Mark Antony. Galba's
edicta to the provinces may have done a little to reduce the
fervour of Vindex's pronouncements, but certainly not very
much. Vindex openly encouraged western opinion, and in
particular the western armed forces, to take a radical view of
what the Roman world required in the way of ethical government from Rome (cf. Sutherland, *Num. Chron.* 1984, pp. 29ff.;
Griffin, *Nero*, p. 186). Galba was, outwardly at least, more
moderate and politically more experienced, and it was Galba
who survived to assume the principate, however briefly.

44. Galba's military expenses in Spain in AD 68

1. Suet. *Galba* 12. 1. Praecesserat de eo (sc. Galba) fama saevitae
simul atque avaritiae, quod civitates Hispaniarum Galliarumque,
quae cunctantius sibi accesserant, gravioribus tributis, quasdam
etiam murorum destructione, punisset et praepositos procuratores-
que supplicio capitis adfecisset cum coniugibus ac liberis; quodque
oblatam a Tarraconensibus e vetere templo Iovis coronam auream
librarum quindecim conflasset, ac tres uncias, quae ponderi deerant,
iussiset exigi.

2. Plut. *Galba* 20. 2. ἀποστάντος δὲ Γάλβα πρῶτος αὐτῷ προσεχώρησε (sc. Otho) τῶν ἡγεμόνων, καὶ φέρων ὅσον εἶχεν ἐν ἐκπώμασι καὶ τραπέζαις ἄργυρον καὶ χρυσὸν ἔδωκε κατακόψαι ποιουμένῳ νόμισμα.

Suet. *Galba* 12. 1. Rumours of Galba's harshness, and of his avarice too, had preceded him, for he had punished those Spanish and Gallic communities which had shown reluctance in joining him with unduly heavy tribute. In some cases he had had their walls pulled down, and had put to death their officials and procurators, together with their wives and children. And there was also the fact that he had melted down a golden crown, weighing fifteen pounds, from the temple of Jupiter, where it had been deposited by the people of Tarraco: this crown, he said, was three ounces short in weight, and he had ordered the deficiency to be made up.

Plut. *Galba* 20. 2. When Galba had revolted, Otho was the first of the provincial governors to join his cause, and he brought all the silver and gold which he possessed in the shape of drinking-cups and tables and gave it to Galba, who was having money coined.

44b   *44c*

a *RIC* I², p. 233, nos. 8f. Aureus and denarius of Spain (Tarraco?), *c.*late spring AD 68. *Obv.* GALBA IMPERATOR, Head of Galba, laureate. *Rev.* LIBERTAS RESTITVTA, Female figure pouring libation.

b *RIC* I², p. 233, nos. 17f. Aureus and denarius of Spain (Tarraco?), *c.* early summer AD 68. *Obv.* GALBA IMP(*erator*), Head of Galba, laureate. *Rev.* GALLIA HISPANIA, Gallia and Hispania, each armed, clasping hands.

c *RIC* I², p. 234, nos. 40f. Aureus and denarius of Spain (Tarraco?), *c.*summer AD 68. *Obv.* GALBA IMPERATOR, Head of Galba, laureate. *Rev.* ROMA RENASC(*ens*), Roma, armed, advancing and holding Victory.

d RIC I², p. 235, nos. 61 f. Aureus and denarius of Spain (Tarraco?), *c.*later summer AD 68. *Obv.* SER(*vius*) GALBA IMP(*erator*) CAESAR AVG(*ustus*) P(*ontifex*) M(*aximus*) TR(*ibunicia*) P(*otestate*), Head of Galba, laureate. *Rev.* S P Q R OB C(*ives*) S(*ervatos*) in oak-wreath.

Galba's adherence to the revolt of Vindex was confirmed in the spring of AD 68 when he accepted salutation as *imperator* by the legion (VI Victrix) under his command (Dio Cass. 63. 23) at Carthago Nova, where, refusing the titles *Caesar* and *Augustus* still held by Nero, he then declared himself *legatus senatus populique Romani* (Suet. *Galba* 10. 1). Suetonius further recorded (*Galba* 10. 2) that Galba next raised additional troops (these included Legio VII Galbiana), exactly as Clodius Macer was doing in Africa (see no. 42 above). From now onwards, therefore, Galba, interdicted from the reception of coinage-supplies from Rome, had himself to provide the means of paying the *stipendia* of two legions (amounting to some three million denarii a year) and of the new auxiliaries now also recruited. Plutarch is our evidence for Galba's production of coinage in Spain. He did not specify where Galba's mint was, but it is reasonable to assume that it was at Tarraco, the site of a busy mint for colonial *aes* earlier in the empire.

The aurei and denarii of this Spanish mint are remarkable both for their quantity and for their variety (cf. *RIC* I², pp. 232–5; for numerous addenda see *NACQT* 1984, pp. 171 ff.). Their types emphasize Spain and its links with the Gaul of Vindex (*b*), and the constant themes of Libertas and Roma Renascens (or Restituta or Victrix) (*a* and *c*). On the earlier issues in this series Galba appears strictly as *imperator*—the result of the legionary salutation in the spring of the year. Later, when he had learned of Nero's death in June, and had met the senatorial delegation at Narbo (Plut. *Galba* 11. 1), sometime about July, he adopted the full titulature of a *de jure* emperor. The operation of a mint for gold and silver in Spain would have presented no problems of bullion-supply, for Spain was outstandingly rich in both metals (cf. Sutherland, *RS*, pp. 104 ff., and *NACQT* 1985, pp. 239 ff.). Nevertheless, the sudden need to pay two legions, with auxiliaries, and to meet the cost of civil officials and services, would certainly have caused some initial strain; and this may have been responsible for an immediate exaction of easily available valuables, including the gold crown weighing fifteen pounds from the temple at Tarraco (in which city the mint probably was). From that weight of gold some 600 aurei could be coined, with a value of 15,000 denarii—the equivalent of a year's pay for about 66 legionary soldiers, and one twenty-fifth, or thereabouts, of Galba's basic military budget (on melting down see Millar, *ERW*, pp. 46f.). Otho's immediate gift of his own domestic gold and silver must have been welcome indeed.

45. Galba and the Clunia oracle

1. Suet. *Galba* 9. 2. Nec diu cunctatus condicionem (cf. no. 43. 1) partim metu partim spe recepit; nam et mandata Neronis de nece sua ad procuratores clam missa deprenderat et confirmabatur cum secundissimis auspiciis et ominibus virginis honestae vaticinatione, tanto magis quod eadem illa carmina sacerdos Iovis Cluniae ex penetrali somnio monitus eruerat ante ducentos annos similiter a fatidica puella pronuntiata. Quorum carminum sententia erat 'oriturum quandoque ex Hispania principem dominumque rerum'.

Suet. *Galba* 9. 2. Galba did not hesitate for long before accepting the proposal, half in fear and half in hope, for he had intercepted orders for his own death sent secretly by Nero to his agents. And he was encouraged by the very favourable auspices and omens of a revered virgin prophetess, and all the more so because the priest of Jupiter at Clunia, under the influence of a trance in his sanctuary, had uttered the same response as that of a young prophetess two hundred years earlier. The purport of the oracular verses was that 'A prince, lord of the world, will one day arise out of Spain'.

45a

a *RIC* I², p. 254, no. 473. Sestertius of Rome, *c.*Dec. AD 68. *Obv.*
SER(*vius*) SVLPI(*cius*) GALBA IMP(*erator*) CAESAR AVG(*ustus*)
P(*ontifex*) M(*aximus*) TR(*ibunicia*) P(*otestate*), Head of Galba,
laureate and draped. *Rev.* HISPANIA CLVNIA SVL(*picia?*), S C,
Galba in military dress, seated on curule chair, holding short
sword and extending right hand to female figure who gives him the
palladium and holds a cornucopia.

Suetonius specifies two reasons as having persuaded Galba to
join Vindex against Nero in the spring of AD 68. The most
urgent was his reported knowledge of Nero's intention to put
him to death. No explicit cause of Nero's hostility towards him
is given, but Galba's wealth (cf. Suet. *Galba* 8. 1) and the fact
that he had been a well known protégé of Tiberius' aged
mother Livia (Suet. *Galba* 5. 2), to whose memory indeed he
devoted a surprising number of coin-types during his own short
principate (*RIC* I², pp. 233 ff., 240 ff., 248, 252; *Diva Augusta* and
Augusta), together with the report that Augustus himself had
foretold Galba's future supremacy (Suet. *Galba* 4. 1), may well
have been factors in Nero's mind. Secondly, there were the
current omens, which always found credulous eyes and ears.
Even Tiberius was said to have told Galba that he would have a
taste of sovereignty (Dio Cass. 64. 1. 1—another link with
Livia?): other omens are duly recounted by Dio and (Galba 8.
2) Suetonius. That which influenced Galba most powerfully,
however, was the repetition of the old prophecy made 200 years
earlier at Clunia, in the distant northern part of Hispania
Tarraconensis, where Galba was staying when he heard of
Vindex's disastrous defeat by Verginius Rufus (Plut. *Galba* 6.
4). 'A *princeps* would one day come out of Spain'; and already
his army had hailed him *imperator*.

Suetonius was obviously correct in estimating the effect of this oracle upon Galba. For about December AD 68, very late in his principate, when his power was weakening and revolution seemed near (Tac. *Hist.* 1. 6), Galba made reference to the Clunia oracle on no less than five distinct varieties of sestertii struck at Rome (*RIC* I², p. 254, nos. 469–73): similar oracular authority for usurpation was to be turned to advantage by Vespasian in Judaea (Josephus, *Bell. Iud.* 3. 401–4 and 4. 623; Tac. *Hist.* 1. 10 and 2. 1). It may be noted, incidentally, that if the Clunia oracle was in fact 200 years old it must have been issued originally for the benefit of Scipio Aemilianus, conqueror of Numantia, becoming thereafter a politically emotive concept of some power in Spain, even if it is not reported in the context of Sertorius and Pompey.

The reverse legend on these fine coins of Galba presents three elements. *Hispania* and *Clunia* are self-explanatory, but it is difficult to see why Galba (shown receiving from Hispania the *palladium* seized from Troy and later to be the symbol of Rome's destined greatness) should be given only his gentile name *Sul*(picius)—unless either that was some imagined part of the oracular pronouncement, or Clunia adopted the additional name *Sulpicia* after Galba's visit there (cf. *Princeton Encyclopedia of Classical Sites* s.v. Clunia). Evidently the revived oracle of the spring was well remembered at the end of the year, when a number of other types also was struck with a significance abruptly different from that of the preceding months. *Honos et Virtus*, *Pietas Augusti*, *Senatus Pietati Augusti*, and the somewhat hopeless *Victoria Imperi Romani* (*RIC* I², pp. 254 f.) all now appeared at this desperate moment: reference to the Clunia oracle was part of an appeal in the dying days of his principate, the final appeal—his adoption of Piso (Tac. *Hist.* 1. 18 f.)—coming but five days before both Galba and Piso were assassinated (Tac. *Hist.* 1. 39 ff.).

46. An unexplained coin-type of Galba

1. Suet. *Galba* 23. Periit (sc. Galba) tertio et septuagesimo aetatis anno, imperii mensis septimo. Senatus, ut primum licitum est, statuam ei decreverat rostratae columnae superstantem in parte fori

qua trucidatus est; sed decretum Vespasianus abolevit, percussores
sibi ex Hispania in Iudaeam submisisse opinatus.

Suet. *Galba* 23. Galba perished in his seventy-third year, and in the
seventh month of his reign. As soon as it was allowed to do so, the
senate voted him a statue standing on a column adorned with ships'
'beaks', to be placed in that part of the forum where he was assassinated. But Vespasian cancelled the decree, for he thought that
Galba had secretly sent men to Judaea to kill him.

46a

a RIC I², p. 256, nos. 507–9. Asses of Rome, *c.*Dec. AD 68. *Obv.*
SER(*vius*) GALBA IMP(*erator*) CAES(*ar*) AVG(*ustus*), TR(*ibunicia*) P(*otestate*), Head of Galba, bare or laureate. *Rev.* S C, Aquila
between two standards, each set on ship's prow.

Suetonius' record of a senatorial decree, after Galba's death, to
erect a statue of him on a *columna rostrata* (for a similar column
celebrating Octavian's victory at Actium cf. *RIC* I², p. 60,
no. 271) suggests that Galba had won a notable naval victory.
No such victory, however, either before or during his principate, has received historical mention. But a naval victory there
must have been. The senatorial decree is firmly recorded: the
honour thus accorded—and previously accorded to Octavian
—was a signal one; and the reverse type of *aes* asses at the end
of AD 68 shows an *aquila* and *vexilla* mounted on ships' prows, a
type not previously seen under the principate.

Possibly Galba gained a naval victory during his two-year
command for the restoration of order in Africa under Claudius (Suet. *Galba* 7. 1), which earned him the *ornamenta triumphalia* (Suet. *Galba* 8. 1). A more recent occasion, however,
and therefore a more plausible one, is to be sought in Galba's

suppression of Clodius Macer's revolt of AD 68 in Africa, in which Macer's naval forces had threatened the steady traffic of the corn-ships from Africa and Egypt to Rome, and a regular coin-type of Macer had shown an *aquila* between *vexilla* (see no. **42** above). Galba's asses could thus show Macer's standards triumphantly mounted on Galba's ships. His victory may not have been a brilliant one, but it maintained the safety of Rome's corn-supply; and it was notable enough to be thought to deserve a monument to a *princeps* recently and humiliatingly assassinated, even though Vespasian later cancelled the senate's decree (on Vespasian and Galba see P. A. Brunt in *JRS* 1977, pp. 104 f.).

It should be noted in passing that Vespasian's action in cancelling the senate's proposed honour to Galba is an argument to be added to those others put forward by C. M. Kraay (*The Aes Coinage of Galba*, pp. 47 ff.) in rejecting the theory of Mattingly (*BMCRE* I, pp. ccxii ff.) that the final group of *aes* in Galba's name was in fact struck by Vespasian as a posthumous mark of honour to Galba.

47. Vitellius and the legions of Germany

1. Tac. *Hist.* 1. 52. Sub ipsas superioris anni kalendas Decembris Aulus Vitellius inferiorem Germaniam ingressus hiberna legionum cum cura adierat: redditi plerisque ordines, remissa ignominia, adlevatae notae . . . Nec consularis legati mensura sed in maius accipiebantur. Et ut Vitellius apud severos humilis, ita comitatem bonitatemque faventes vocabant (of AD 69).

2. Tac. *Hist.* 1. 56. Nocte quae kalendas Ianuarias secuta est in coloniam Agrippinensem aquilifer quartae legionis epulanti Vitellio nuntiat quartam et duetvicensimam legiones . . . in senatus ac populi Romani verba iurasse. Id sacramentum inane visum: occupari nutantem fortunam et offerri principem placuit (of AD 69).

3. Tac. *Hist.* 1. 57. . . . Fabius Valens . . . die postero coloniam Agrippinensem . . . ingressus imperatorem Vitellium consalutavit . . . et superior exercitus, speciosis senatus populique Romani nominibus relictis, tertium nonas Ianuarias Vitellio accessit (of AD 69).

4. Suet. *Vitellius* 8. 2. Consentiente deinde etiam superioris provinciae exercitu ... cognomen Germanici delatum ab universis cupide recepit, Augusti distulit, Caesaris in perpetuum recusavit.

Tac. *Hist.* 1. 52. Just before 1 December of the preceding year Aulus Vitellius had entered Lower Germany, approaching the winter quarters of the legions with a careful policy. Rank was restored to most of those who had lost it, punishments were remitted, disgrace was lightened ... All this was taken at its maximum value, and not merely as the behaviour of a consular governor. The strait-laced might think Vitellius undignified, but the soldiers were pleased, and spoke of his easy good nature.

Tac. *Hist.* 1. 56. On the night of 1–2 January the standard-bearer of the Fourth Legion entered the colony of Cologne while Vitellius was at dinner and announced that the Fourth and Twenty-second Legions had sworn loyalty to the senate and people of Rome. That oath did not seem to amount to much; and Vitellius decided to swing fortune in his own favour and to seize power as princeps.

Tac. *Hist.* 1. 57. Next day Fabius Valens entered the colony of Cologne and saluted Vitellius as emperor ... and the army of Upper Germany, abandoning the fine but empty concepts of 'the senate and people of Rome', joined Vitellius' cause on 3 January.

Suet. *Vitellius* 8. 2. When the army of Upper Germany also sided with him, ... the universal offer of the *cognomen* 'Germanicus' was made to Vitellius. He accepted it eagerly, while deferring that of 'Augustus': that of 'Caesar' he refused permanently.

47a   **47c**

a *RIC* I², p. 268, no. 12. Aureus of (?)Tarraco, *c.*January–June AD 69. *Obv.* A(*ulus*) VITELLIVS IMP(*erator*) GERMANICVS,

Head of Vitellius, laureate. *Rev.* SECVRITAS IMP(*eratoris*) GER-
MAN(*ici*), Securitas seated with sceptre by torch leaning against
garlanded and lighted altar.

b *RIC* I², p. 270, no. 47. Denarius of Lugdunum, *c.*March–July
AD 69. *Obv.* A(*ulus*) VITELLIVS IMP(*erator*) GERMANICVS,
Head of Vitellius, laureate. *Rev.* FIDES EXERCITVVM, Clasped
right hands.

c *RIC* I², p. 271, no. 64. Aureus of Lugdunum, *c.*March–July AD 69.
Obv. A(*ulus*) VITELLIVS GER(*manicus*) IMP(*erator*) AVG(*ustus*)
P(*ontifex*) MAX(*imus*) TR(*ibunicia*) P(*otestate*), Head of Vitellius,
laureate. *Rev.* CONSENSVS EXERCITVVM, Mars advancing
with spear, aquila, and vexillum.

d *RIC* I², p. 271, no. 68. Denarius of Rome, *c.*late April–December
AD 69. *Obv.* A(*ulus*) VITELLIVS GERMANICVS IMP(*erator*),
Head of Vitellius, bare. *Rev.* IVPPITER VICTOR, Jupiter seated,
holding Victory and sceptre.

According to Suetonius (*Vitellius* 7) the legions of Lower
Germany were not enthusiastic in their reception of Vitellius
when he was sent by Galba as their commander. But Vitellius'
assiduous efforts to win their favour by all possible means soon
prevailed, and resulted in his eager acceptance of the proffered
cognomen 'Germanicus' (of which, incidentally, the sequential
abbreviation to *German*, *Germa*, *Germ*, and *Ger* provides valu-
able guidance for the chronology of his coinage; cf. *RIC* I²,
p. 262). Having already been saluted as *imperator*, he now
became *A. Vitellius Germanicus imperator*. It was Mattingly who
observed (*BMCRE* I, pp. ccxxii f.) in relation to the mint of
Rome—and his observation is relevant also to the majority of
Vitellius' coinage-issues from Spain and Gaul—that Vitellius
(or those in charge of his coinage) showed a preference for the
style *Imp Germanicus* over that of *Germanicus Imp*, which was
certainly the normal titular sequence (cf. the Neronian titula-
tures in *RIC* I², p. 155). This abnormal inversion causes us,
therefore, to interpret *Imp Germanicus* in the sense (acutely
understood by Mattingly) of 'imperator by the will of the
armies in the German provinces'.

The coins with this abnormal titulature thus seem to reflect
accurately the surge of support which Vitellius received, first
from the legions of Lower Germany, and then almost at once

from those of Upper Germany, in January AD 69 (see G. E. F. Chilver in *JRS* 1957, pp. 29–38, and more recently K. Wellesley, *The Long Year AD 69* (London, 1975), pp. 34–7). It is noticeable, however, that the mint of Rome, where Vitellius' coinage mostly post-dated that of Spain and Gaul, settled down to the normal *Germanicus Imp* sequence after beginning with *Imp Germanicus*. Presumably the traditional convention of Rome was strong enough to prevail; and possibly sentiment at Rome was reluctant to acknowledge the influence of the legions in Germany in establishing Vitellius at Rome. As for the title 'Augustus', deferred according to Suetonius, this appeared on very rare coinage-issues in Spain early in AD 69, on isolated *Ger Imp* issues in Gaul in mid-69 (*c*), on fairly numerous issues in Rome from mid-69 onwards—in all these cases on aurei and denarii—and without exception on the *aes* of Rome throughout the period *c*.late April–December 69. The normal titular usage thus prevailed finally at Rome. The title 'Caesar', however, never appeared on Vitellius' coinage at any of his mints: Suetonius' statement was absolutely correct.

48. Vitellius and the war in Judaea

1. Tac. *Hist.* 1. 10. Bellum Iudaicum Flavius Vespasianus (ducem eum Nero delegerat) tribus legionibus administrabat (of late AD 68).

2. Tac. *Hist.* 2. 4. Profligaverat bellum Iudaicum Vespasianus, obpugnatione Hierosolymorum reliqua ... Tres, ut supra memoravimus, ipsi Vespasiano legiones erant, exercitae bello (of spring AD 69).

3. Tac. *Hist.* 2. 78. Grande id (i.e. the omen of the resurgent tree) prosperumque consensu haruspicum et summa claritudo iuveni admodum Vespasiano promissa, sed primo triumphalia et consulatus (i.e. of AD 51) et Iudaicae victoriae decus implesse fidem ominis videbatur (of late spring AD 69).

Tac. *Hist.* 1. 10. Flavius Vespasianus, chosen as general by Nero, was conducting the Jewish war with three legions.

Tac. *Hist.* 2. 4. Vespasian had broken the back of the Jewish war, and only the siege of Jerusalem remained ... As I have already noted, Vespasian had three legions, well trained in war.

Tac. *Hist.* 2. 78. That seemed a fine and favourable omen, as the seers all agreed, and although he was quite young Vespasian seemed to be destined for a most brilliant future. But at first his triumphal distinctions, his consulship, and the renown of his Jewish victory seemed to have fulfilled the promise of the prophecy.

48a

a *RIC* I², p. 274, no. 123. Sestertius of Rome, *c.*late spring AD 69. *Obv.* A(*ulus*) VITELLIVS GERMANICVS IMP(*erator*) AVG(*ustus*) P(*ontifex*) M(*aximus*) TR(*ibunicia*) P(*otestate*), Head of Vitellius, laureate. *Rev.* VICTORIA AVGVSTI, S C, Victory, naked to waist, with foot on helmet, inscribing OB CIVES SERV(*atos*) on round shield fixed to palm-tree.

Josephus records (*Bell. Iud.* 3. 1. 3) that the three legions under Vespasian's command for the war in Judaea were V Macedonica, X Fretensis, and XV Apollinaris. By the spring of AD 69 these had broken the main strength of Jewish resistance. Vespasian could thus be credited with *Iudaicae victoriae decus*, and could leave the final stage of the war—the reduction of Jerusalem—to Titus, while he himself prepared to move against Vitellius (Josephus, *Bell. Iud.* 4. 11. 5). Suetonius' *Vitellius* contains no record of the Jewish war under that emperor— most eyes had naturally been fixed on events in Rome and Italy—but Vitellius' coinage contains a clear and interesting reflection of it.

Fine sestertii struck in Rome, and in some quantity, in the middle of AD 69 with the unabbreviated title *Germanicus* (see no. **47** above) show Victory fixing a triumphal shield to a palm-tree. C. M. Kraay pointed out in an unpublished paper that, while a palm-*branch* had been the symbol of victory since early Republican days, a palm-*tree* was to become a standard symbol of Judaea, as Vespasian's subsequent *Iudaea Capta* sestertii so clearly show (cf. *BMCRE* II, pl. 20). Vitellius' sestertii with *Victoria Augusti*, Victory, and palm-tree therefore officially recorded and celebrated Vespasian's successes in Judaea as having been gained (according to normal theory and practice) under the auspices of Vitellius as the holder of supreme *imperium*.

49. Vitellius and *Concordia*

1. Tac. *Hist.* 3. 68. Nec quisquam adeo rerum humanarum immemor quem non commoveret illa facies, Romanum principem (sc. Vitellium) . . . per populum, per urbem exire de imperio . . . In sua contione Vitellius pauca et praesenti maestitiae congruentia locutus—cedere se pacis et rei publicae causa . . .—exolutum a latere pugionem, velut ius necis vitaeque civium, reddebat. Aspernante consule, reclamantibus qui in contione adstiterant, ut in aede Concordiae positurus insignia imperii . . . discessit (of Dec. 17 AD 69).

2. Suet. *Vitellius* 15. 4. Tunc solutum a latere pugionem consuli primum, deinde illo recusante magistratibus ac mox senatoribus singulis porrigens, nullo recipiente, quasi in aede Concordiae positurus abscessit. Sed quibusdam adclamantibus ipsum esse Concordiam, rediit nec solum retinere se ferrum affirmavit, verum etiam Concordiae recipere cognomen.

Tac. *Hist.* 3. 68. No one was so unmindful of human affairs as to be unmoved by that sight—the Roman emperor departing from his seat of power through the people, through Rome . . . Vitellius' public address contained few words, and those few suitable to the sadness of the occasion: he said that he was yielding on account of peace, and of the state . . . He unfastened the dagger at his side, and offered it back, as if it was the symbol of his lawful right of life and death over the citizenry. The consul refused to accept it, and his surrounding audience replied by shouting: so he then departed . . . to place the outward symbols of his power in the temple of Concord.

Suet. *Vitellius* 15. 4. Vitellius then unfastened the dagger from his side. He offered it first to the consul, who refused it, and then to the magistrates, and presently to individual senators. None would accept it, and he then made to leave, with the intention of placing it in the temple of Concord. But some shouted that he himself was Concord, and he came back, saying not only that he would keep the weapon, but also that he would take for himself the cognomen 'Concordia'.

49a

49b

a RIC I², p. 271, no. 66. Denarius of Rome, spring AD 69. *Obv.* A(*ulus*) VITELLIVS GERMANICVS IMP(*erator*), Head of Vitellius, bare. *Rev.* CONCORDIA P(*opuli*) R(*omani*), Concordia seated, holding patera and cornucopia.

b RIC I², p. 276, no. 162. Dupondius of Rome, later in AD 69. *Obv.* A(*ulus*) VITELLIVS GERMA(*nicus*) IMP(*erator*) AVG(*ustus*) P(*ontifex*) M(*aximus*) TR(*ibunicia*) P(*otestate*), Head of Vitellius, laureate. *Rev.* CONCORDIA AVGVSTI, S C, Concordia seated as above, but in front of lighted altar.

The growth and the political manipulation of the concept of *concordia* has been searchingly analysed by Barbara Levick (*Scripta . . . Sutherland*, pp. 217 ff.). Her conclusion, based on the abundant literary evidence of the Roman republic and empire, is that *concordia*, originally reflecting senatorial effort to impose an orderly political structure upon the other classes of Roman society, was later widened (especially by Cicero) in an attempt to create a genuine partnership between senate, *equites*, and *plebs*, and that its significance was once more changed under the principate, when the emperors had to maintain a balanced loyalty not only between these elements, but with the army as well, if the state was to preserve its stability. *Concordia*, moreover, was by now all too frequently invoked when *discordia* was present or threatened.

This interpretation is consonant with the evidence of the imperial coinage. It was during the civil wars of AD 68–70 that Concordia, without qualification, first appeared as a concept on the coinage (the temple of Concordia, with no explanatory legend, had appeared on the coinage of Tiberius; cf. *RIC* I², pp. 97 f., nos. 55, 61, 67, and Levick, op. cit., pp. 224 f.). In those civil wars Concordia was first seen on the seemingly nostalgic 'Augustus' issues struck probably in Spain *c.*68–9 (*RIC* I², p. 211, no. 91) and then on the very rare 'Gallic Revolt' series from Lower Germany *c.*69–70 (*RIC* I², p. 214, nos. 132, 134). Qualified, as *Concordia Hispaniarum et Galliarum*, or *Orb*(is) *Ter*(rarum), it appeared on the 'anonymous' series of Spain and Gaul in 68–9 (*RIC* I², pp. 204, no. 15; 207, no. 41) and as *Concordia Provinciarum* or *Praetorianorum* on the southern Gaulish(?) 'anonymous' series of 69 (*RIC* I², p. 213, nos. 118 f.). Galba's gold and silver coinage adopted the concept of *Concordia Provinciarum* in 68 in Spain and Gaul and thereafter at Rome (*RIC* I², pp. 234, no. 35 etc.; 237 f., nos. 104, 117–20, 125 f.; 241, nos. 149, 180); and his *aes* of Rome introduced the newly qualified *Concord*(ia) *Aug*(usti) (*RIC* I², p. 248, nos. 339–45). The concept of Concordia was absent from Otho's coinage, but it reappeared on that of Vitellius, whom Tacitus (cf. *Hist.* 1. 56) and Suetonius describe as being so conscious of the function of this pacifying quality that he proposed depositing the *signa imperii* (not defined by either historian) in the temple of Concordia before he abdicated, and accepted the *cognomen* 'Concordia'. His gold and silver coinage of Rome had already introduced the newly qualified concept of *Concordia P*(opuli) *R*(omani) (*RIC* I², p. 271, no. 55 etc.; see (*a*)), and his *aes* had continued the *Concordia Augusti* (see *b*) previously introduced by Galba. The significance of Concordia had thus veered quite away from its original sense of harmony between the principal social orders. With *Consensus Exercituum* in the background in Spain and Gaul (*RIC* I², p. 269, nos. 20–6, 40 etc.), Concordia now appealed for harmony in the heart of the state, the entire Roman people, at whose head Vitellius was prepared to stand forth as her human agent, if necessary even by abdication.

50. The cost of civil warfare in AD 68–9

1. Suet. *Div. Vesp.* 8. 1 and 4. Talis tantaque cum fama in urbem reversus (sc. Vespasianus) acto de Iudaeis triumpho consulatus octo veteri addidit; suscepit et censuram ac per totum imperii tempus nihil habuit antiquius quam prope afflictam nutantemque rem p. stabilire primo, deinde et ornare ... Achaiam, Lyciam, Rhodum, Byzantium, Samum libertate adempta, item Trachiam Ciliciam et Commagenen dicionis regiae usque ad id tempus in provinciarum formam redegit.

2. Suet. *Div. Vesp.* 16. 1 and 3. Sola est, in qua merito culpetur, pecuniae cupiditas. Non enim contentus omissa sub Galba vectigalia revocasse, nova et gravia addidisse, auxisse tributa provinciis, non-nullis et duplicasse, negotiationes quoque vel privato pudendas propalam exercuit ... Sunt contra qui opinentur ad manubias et rapinas necessitate compulsum summa aerarii fiscique inopia, de qua testificatus sit initio statim principatus, professus 'quadrin-genties milies opus esse, ut res p. stare posset'.

Suet. *Div. Vesp.* 8. 1 and 4. Such was the man, and such his reputa-tion, when Vespasian returned to Rome. He duly celebrated his Jewish triumph, and went on to add eight further consulships to that which he had gained earlier. He also assumed the censorship, and for the whole of his reign held nothing to be of greater importance than to steady a battered and tottering state, and then to embellish it ... He deprived Achaea, Lycia, Rhodes, Byzantium and Samos of their freedom and reduced them to provincial status, like Trachian Cilicia and Commagene, which until then had been client kingdoms.

Suet. *Div. Vesp.* 16. 1 and 3. For one thing alone he might be justifi-ably criticized—his avarice. He was not content with reimposing taxes lifted by Galba, or with imposing new and heavy taxes, or with increasing (even sometimes doubling) provincial tribute. He openly carried out bargaining which would be shameful even for a man in private life ... Some, on the other hand, think that acute lack of funds in the public and the imperial treasury was the spur which drove him to spoil and seizure. He gave evidence of this at the very beginning of his principate when he declared that the state needed forty thousand million (sc. sesterces) if it was to stand firm.

Suetonius gives a balanced and sympathetic account of Vespasian, the unaristocratic but greatly experienced general whose chief object as *princeps* was to restore the shaken and impoverished Roman state. There was a sheer lack of money. Too many armies in too many areas had been paid to destroy too much. Vespasian's estimate of the need of 40,000 million sesterces (more easily comprehended as 10,000 million denarii or 400 million aurei) might perhaps have to be reduced to a tenth of that figure if the reading *quadringenties* were replaced by that of *quadragies*. Even so, the deficit was enormous, and one wonders how Vespasian estimated it. Perhaps it was a rule-of-thumb calculation of the proceeds of a given number of years of taxation, such as five (as after an earthquake; see no. **18**), or ten, or (cf. K. Hopkins in *JRS* 1980, pp. 119) even more. In any case, not only must mints work at maximum pressure, but large supplies of coinage-metal had first to be obtained. The supply-lines for the principal source of gold and silver bullion—that of Spain—had been totally interrupted by the revolt of Galba, with Otho, in that province (cf. Sutherland, *NACQT* 1985, pp. 239f.). Immense quantities of gold were normally furnished to the central government of Rome by the Spanish mines (cf. L. C. West, *Imperial Roman Spain: the Objects of Trade* (Oxford, Blackwell, 1929), p. 50), the elder Pliny specifically recording (*NH* 33. 78) that 20,000 pounds' weight was extracted annually, by processes carefully described, from Lusitania alone. And Spain was very rich in silver too: the great mines near Carthago Nova described by Polybius were still being worked in the time of Strabo (3. 2. 9), and there were many others (cf. West, op. cit., pp. 50f.). Nor were other parts of the empire devoid of gold and silver, although Spain was certainly the richest. Once in power, Vespasian controlled all such sources. He had other, and administrative, means of raising money as well. As *censor* in AD 73 (an office duly noted on the coinage of that year; cf. *RIC* II, pp. 21f.) he could record in detail the resources of the empire. The taxes which he now reimposed included the *quadragensima* (2½% customs duty) remitted by Galba on goods entering Gaul (cf. *RIC* I², p. 236, nos. 77–84; p. 239, no. 134; p. 246, nos. 293, 296; on this remission see S. J. de Laet, *Portorium* (Gent, 1949), pp. 170–3). His re-provincialization of previously 'free' provinces and areas brought in an added yield of taxation. His great municipal reform in Spain (cf. R. K. McElderry, *JRS* 1918, pp. 53ff.; Pliny, *NH* 3. 30; Sutherland, *The Romans in Spain*, pp. 183ff.;

and now N. Mackie, *Local Administration in Roman Spain, AD 14-212* (BAR Internat. Ser. 172, Oxford, 1983), pp. 215-19) exempted newly enfranchised communities from *tributum capitis* but made them liable to indirect taxes at a time when the Spanish economy was growing vigorously.

Pecuniae cupiditas this may have been, but there was an urgent *necessitas*. The variety of measures which Vespasian took enabled him to coin, fairly profusely, in gold and silver (as well, of course, as in *aes*) from the mint of Rome from AD 69 onwards, as well as from mints certainly or probably to be recognized as Tarraco (69-?71), Lugdunum (69-?73), Byzantium and Ephesus (69-71), Antioch (69 and 72-3; cf. Tac. *Hist.* 2. 82), and elsewhere (*RIC* II, pp. 1 ff., 15-61). Presumably coinage was produced wherever bullion could be found for it: this initially decentralized pattern of mints from west to east would have been due in part to the inability of Rome to supply, unaided, an empire-wide coinage at a time when frontier defences and war damage, in Italy especially, has to be repaired and gratuities paid to retired soldiers. For example, Vespasian reduced the strength of the Praetorian Guard from the sixteen cohorts of Vitellius to the Augustan figure of nine, and (Suet. *Div. Vesp.* 8. 2) he disbanded large parts of Vitellius' regular army.

INDEX

I. Personal Names

II. General